SAM SHEPARD

SAM SHEPARD

The Life and Work of an American Dreamer

ELLEN OUMANO

St. Martin's Press
New York

Excerpts from "Camp Shepard: Exploring the Geography of Character," by Scott Christopher Wren. *West Coast Plays,* 1980, reprinted by permission of the author.

Excerpts from "Clues in a Memory," *American Dreams: The Imagination of Sam Shepard,* ed. Bonnie Marranca. New York: *Performing Arts Journal,* 1981, reprinted by permission of the author.

Excerpts from "Metaphors, Mad Dogs, and Old Time Cowboys: Interview With Sam Shepard," by Kenneth Chubb and the editors of *Theatre Quarterly,* reprinted in *American Dreams: The Imagination of Sam Shepard,* ed. Bonnie Marranca. New York: *Performing Arts Journal,* 1981, reprinted by permission of the publishers.

Excerpts from *The Off-Off Broadway Book,* by Albert Poland and Bruce Mailman. New York: Bobbs-Merrill, 1972, reprinted by permission of the author.

Excerpts from *On the Road With Bob Dylan,* by Larry Sloman. New York: Bantam Books, 1978, reprinted by permission of the author.

Excerpts from "The Saga of Sam Shepard," by Robert Coe. *The New York Times,* November 23, 1980, reprinted by permission of the author.

Design by Amy Bernstein

Library of Congress Cataloging in Publication Data

Oumano, Ellen.
   Sam Shepard: the life and work of an American dreamer.

   1. Shepard, Sam 1943–   . 2. Authors, American—
20th century—Biography.   3. Actors—United States—
Biography.   I. Title.
PS3569.H394Z8   1986   812'.54[B]   85-25111
ISBN 312-69839-9

First Edition
10 9 8 7 6 5 4 3 2 1

This book is dedicated to the following people:
Yamuna Becker; Nancy Brand; Robert Cook;
Yogi Amrit Desai; Eugene Pascal; Eric Roth;
Lawrence, Robert, Rose, and Jack Shamis;
and Sudevi (Jane Wright), for reasons they will
understand. Thank you.

Acknowledgments

I wish to thank the following people without whose
generous assistance this book could not have been written:
Tom Allen; my agent, Geri Thoma of the Elaine Markson
Agency; John Starstad and Brian McKenzie of the
University of California, Davis campus; Joyce Aaron, Nestor
Almendros, Tony Barsha, Robert Coe, Peter Craig, Art
d'Lugoff, Michael Feingold, George Ferencz, Jack Gelber,
Burton Greenhouse, Wynn Handman, Bill Hart, Skip
LaPlante, Jacques Levy, Harry Mann, Charles Mingus III,
Robert Monticello, Kevin O'Connor, Albert Poland, Don
Plumley, Michael Roloff, Gary Sinise, Larry Sloman,
Michael Smith, Peter Stampfel, Paul Sylbert, and Scott Wren.

There are more spells than your commonplace magicians ever dreamed up.

—Joseph Conrad, Victory

There is a mysterious identity of essence between the principle of theatre and that of alchemy. Where alchemy, through its symbols, is the spiritual Double of an operation which functions only on the level of real matter, the theatre must also be considered as the Double, not of this direct, everyday reality of which it is gradually being reduced to a mere inert replica . . . but of another archetypal and dangerous reality, a reality of which the Principles, like dolphins, once they have shown their heads, hurry to dive back into the obscurity of the deep.

—Antonin Artaud

Begin the play. . . .
Let these our walls disclose the mysteries hidden.
Hindrance there's none, for magic is our aim,
The arras shrivels up, as if in flame;
The wall is cleft, folds back, and has become
The vista of a theater, deep, inviting,
Embracing us in its mysterious lighting.

—Goethe, Faust

The class of '64 held a reunion on Tuesday night. The immediate reason was to celebrate the 41st birthday of one of its famous sons, Sam Shepard. But in a broader sense it was an occasion for the theatrical rebels of 20 years ago to remember, to take stock.

Shepard, of course, was not there—the former resident of the East Village now eschewing America east of the Mississippi—but Lanford Wilson, Leonard Melfi, Crystal Field, Maria Irene Fornes, Kevin O'Connor, Ralph Lee and others were. Mr. Melfi

even brought a birthday present for the absent Shepard: a wine-
skin. "It fits his pioneer spirit," the playwright said. "And be-
sides, he's the new Gary Cooper."

—The New York Times, *Sunday, November 15, 1984*

x———

────────── ONE ─

Writer of more than forty plays, three volumes of prose, and several screenplays (including *Paris, Texas,* voted Best Film at Cannes in 1984), winner of the Pulitzer Prize for *Buried Child* and ten Obies (awards given by the *Village Voice* for distinguished achievement off- and off-off-Broadway), and Academy Award nominee for Best Supporting Actor for *The Right Stuff,* Sam Shepard is his own greatest invention. A true American hero, Shepard personifies our cultural ambiguity: yearning for transcendence yet hypnotized by our crassest myths. America values her statesmen, philosophers, and artists, but she mythologizes her gunslingers, her men of action, says cop-writer Joseph Wambaugh—and Shepard, at bottom, is a man of action. He has played many of our cultural roles: cowboy, construction worker, rock musician, drug addict, writer, actor; and has now metamorphosed into the ultimate American fantasy figure—Movie Star—thereby achieving the status of one of the myths that populate his own virile, charged, and glitteringly mysterious plays. But legends die fast and hard in America, landscape of abundant disposables. Shepard is well aware of this—he has decried materialism and creeping mechanization often enough in his writing—so it is a perfect irony that he is fast becoming a Hollywood icon, that peculiarly American object of reverence and contempt—a being about whom people want to know more than they have a right to—with the life span of a shooting star.

Shepard's defense of rock 'n' roll legend Bob Dylan could be even more accurately applied to himself: "He's made himself up from scratch. That is, from the things he had around him and inside him. [He] is an invention of his own mind. The point isn't to figure him out but to take him in. He gets to you anyway, so why not just take him in?"[1]

Shepard's got a tattoo of a sliver moon, a hawk moon, on his hand. He and Patti Smith got them together "during my wayward youth," as he told writer Robert Coe. Shepard has written of the tattoo as something to be earned, when his "animal spirit was king. He'd cracked through. Now he had his chops." He writes similarly of his birth month: "Hawk Moon month November my birth month month of cold set in month when secrets start to whisper on the mesa . . ."[2] as if the hawk moon signaled something portentous.

It's part of the personal mythology he's constructed for himself—Son of the West, inheritor of a divided nature: "It's a real thing, double nature. I think we're split in a much more devastating way than psychology can ever reveal. It's not so cute. Not some little thing we can get over. It's something we've got to live with."[3] The division is not psychological but archetypal, characterized by the American male who wants savagery and innocence, who yearns to be on the road at the same time he wants to settle down, who wants utter freedom yet feels his responsibilities. Shepard senses all these conflicts within himself and knows his is a classic dilemma. He wants to be a star, but he doesn't want to open himself to ridicule.

But he is different from the movie stars who *seem* to contain unresolved mysteries, who exist as blank screens for our fantastical projections. Shepard really *is* a man of mystery, a man who has met his dark side: "I've always been pulled towards darkness. Toward black. Toward death. Toward the South. Good."[4]

Compare Shepard's face with that of Richard Gere in *Days of Heaven*. When Gere gazes across the wheat fields, accomplished actor as he may be, we know he's seeing wheat; when we look in Shepard's eyes, something more is going on, he's doing more than acting (perhaps he's writing *Buried Child*). Shepard is continually encountering his unregenerate darker self and attempting to transmute what is leaden into the gold of his art. In the characters about which he writes and those he plays, he is searching for a role as he discovers himself: "You are working out yourself," he has described it in an interview with the *Los Angeles Herald Examiner*. "You're asking questions and thinking about where your last play left off. And you don't always come up with the answers.

"Most writers are cooking up ideas that will make their next projects, but the ideas aren't vital to them.

"I'm driven by a deep dissatisfaction. What you accomplish in your work always falls short of the possibilities you know are sneaking around. The work never gets easier. It gets harder and more provocative. And as it gets harder you are continually reminded there is more to accomplish. It's like digging for gold. And when you find the vein, you know there's a lot more where that came from."

Long ago, Shepard said he would rather be a rock 'n' roll star than a playwright, but Shepard's innate discipline, his love of work and instinctive need for privacy, are better suited for the behind-the-scenes life of a writer. Though he may be ambivalent, movie stardom is catching him, but all the rock 'n' roll stars want to be film stars anyway, so, in a sense, his early fantasy has been fulfilled. In fact, Shepard seems to have fulfilled all kinds of fantasies—his and ours, as well. He seems to have everything: an American aristocrat's face and body, great talent, intelligence, and allure, and from these gifts he has drawn good work, money, fame, respect, and love. But his has been no charmed life, and for Shepard and many others, writing can be a kind of salvation: "If I hadn't had that, I don't know what would have happened to me," he's said. Writing is Shepard's alchemy, enabling him to draw from the undifferentiated chaos of the unconscious and to transform what is negative into a positive and fruitful orientation—art.

Born Samuel Shepard Rogers in 1943, Shepard grew up in southern California—his youth was a more rural and tougher version of *American Graffiti*—enamored with the Wild West but nurtured by the car culture, movies, rock 'n' roll, and the ersatz spiritualism which sprouted like weeds out of the culture of post–World War II America: a compost made up of an earthy pioneer spirit which had rigidified into a collective lifestyle of rampant consumerism. America had lost its god and fallen into social and psychological crisis, into a void. Shepard learned remarkably early that vacuums exert a great deal of energy, pulling toward them whatever will fill the emptiness. He observed this spiritual need in himself and in the surrounding culture, and from his observations and his need seems to come the impetus to write, to work it out in the most renewing way possible.

Shepard's plays have little in common with literary tradition. He offers his audience no purging of emotions, no catharsis according to Aristotelian laws of drama. He is a playwright of jazz and rock 'n' roll, at times spouting wild, original verbiage, at others, lean, sullen, and laid back. We sense in his work intimations of a vague longing, a sense of something missing and missed. It's a profound disappointment with which we identify, so as we are not alienated by the illogicalities, the abrupt switches of characters and situations, the ambiguous symbolism refusing to yield up clear-cut meanings, the problematic endings: "I never know when to end a play," Shepard told *The New York Times*. "I'd just as soon not end anything. But you have to stop at some point just to let people out of the theater. A resolution isn't an ending; it's a strangulation."

Shepard's writing doesn't tell us *about* life; it is fragments of life observed, pieced together and transformed into fragments of all our lives, perceived not through the intellect but through the ear, like music, through the eye, like visual art, and through the heart.

Shepard's father was a drummer and Shepard himself plays a variety of instruments. He played drums and recorded with the Sixties country-psychedelic group the Holy Modal Rounders; once reviewed an Ornette Coleman album for the "Riffs" section of the *Village Voice;* has sat in with several free-form jazz groups; wrote the scores to *Pecos Bill* and *Tooth of Crime;* played drums in the bands accompanying many productions of his plays; and generally seems to have greater rapport with musicians than with theater people. Music clearly shapes and distinguishes both his subject and style. In *Drama Review,* he elucidated the connection between music and his writing process: "I've practiced Jack Kerouac's discovery of jazz-sketching with words . . . following the exact same principles as a musician does when he's jamming. After periods of this kind of practice, I get the haunting sense that something in me writes but it's not necessarily me. . . . This identical experience happened to me once when I was playing drums with the Holy Modal Rounders."[5]

Shepard is a cool king of rhythm, and, like a good drummer, he can lock into any style. He knows rhythm unifies a piece of art because a rhythm is a structure, and things must be structured. Everything is rhythm because everything is form. Without form, there is no life.

His fractured rhythms, composed of speed, bursts of monologue, sudden switches, gearings down to quiet loneliness, are the subtle indications of the rhythms of our lives. "Words are tools of imagery in motion," he says. His rhythms create the unarticulated meanings; they are the glue that holds together

Shepard the playwright, the musician, the artist, the screen-writer, the movie star, the cowboy, the family man. They are the bond that holds us to him.

We are drawn, as well, to the off-to-one-side stance of his characters—both those he writes and those he plays. These are men who participate in life but always reserve a part of themselves, the part that observes the self and the other. Shepard's split of consciousness mirrors our own essential ambiguity about our experience. Again, Shepard's analysis of someone else—in this case the magic of Buster Keaton—could just as well be applied to himself: "You see him in action and you notice it's a double action with two opposites happening simultaneously. You notice the face just being a face and nothing more or less than a face and for that reason it becomes more of a face but don't worry."[6]

Shepard's world and his persona are many more times than "double." In the introduction to *The Unseen Hand* he wrote, "Everybody's caught up in a fractured world that they can't even see. What's happening to them is unfathomable but they have a suspicion. Something unseen is working on them. Using them. They have no power and all the time they believe they're controlling the situation." The theater, then, becomes an arena for ritual healing, where the playwright has set into motion an integrating experience of communal energy between the performance and the spectator.

Shepard is searching, not for effect, but to wrest some kind of transcendence over this life, at once ordinary and overwhelming. His early years were difficult, requiring him to draw upon his own innate reserves of strength. The lack of a strong, consistent father made his struggle to establish an individual identity a life-long theme, if not an obsession. The key to understanding Shepard is to recognize that he dealt with what was given him in the most positive way possible: He seems to have always known that in order to be fully human, he must journey into what is dark, hidden, and powerful—into the unconscious —and bring his demons out into the light of consciousness, harnessing their psychic force and transforming it into Eros, the principle of creativity and of love. Shepard has found that he can do this through his work.

The myth of Hercules and the Hydra describes the universal task that Shepard has recognized and taken on. Hercules is summoned by a town to kill the Hydra, a multi-headed beast who lives in a cave. He shoots arrows into the cave at first because he's afraid to enter the dark and encounter this unknown monster. Angered, the Hydra comes out of the cave, and in his fright, Hercules forgets that if you chop off one head of the Hydra, three grow in its place. On the verge of collapse and overwhelmed, Hercules gets on one knee, signifying respect for the powerful and divine, which the Hydra represents, and lifts the heads into the sunlight, thereby allowing all but one to dry up and dissolve. The lesson, of course, is that one must have respect for the forces that are hidden from our awareness and the courage to confront our own darkness and bring it out into illumination. Like the Hydra, the unconscious can never be killed. Nor should it be killed. It must be integrated into the conscious if it is to become the source of one's power and creativity.

The unconscious is not individual, it is collective; it is not psychological, it is archetypal. Because he actively engages his unconscuous, Shepard's themes and images seem to bubble up in a kind of concentrated, prolific outpouring, from a source deep within instinctual memory: the feeling for land and water, the struggle between father and son, the sense of heredity as both a blessing and a curse, the odyssey in search of individual identity, the power wars within families and within oneself. Whatever has been painful and difficult in his life has been both a lesson and a wellspring for his work. His characters—cowboys, Indians, gangsters, outlaws, movie stars, rock stars, magic men, freaks, now even his own film star persona —are America's comic-book version of the gods of Olympus, embodying and performing our individual and collective dreams and nightmares. These characters are our cultural heroes, our religion. Shepard shows them to us in order that we experience a reflection of ourselves, in order that we may see how we fill our void with unconscious contents, our projections, our fantasies.

Shepard is above all a worker at life, with a gift to "write as fluidly as anyone thought or spoke," says Charles Mingus III, Shepard's friend in the early New York days. "He was the most disciplined writer I've ever known or imagined could even exist, because for him writing is very, very real. Other writers are cramming the words out and can't get them on paper fast enough. He can see it at a distance, coming on to it with—I don't know if it's calm—but at least with some facility—like you would have a conversation and put it on paper. He would sit down with a stack of paper—not like in the movies, balling it up—he'd write it. Then the next thing he would deal with it, and that's really very important. The point is you commit to the words, you know what you mean, and you mean what you say, and you say it. That's as close to sculpture and real time as you can get. That is what is theater—moving sculpture. I think he was aware of mastering stagecraft. He would look at it like a carpentry job, like plumbing. I just have an image of him sitting down at a small but adequate table with a sturdy typewriter and a pile of papers and then a box—a ream of paper—and a play or two plays. Just neat and simple and clean. Basic and that's it. From A to Z—the play is done."

Shepard's persona is unified and powerfully attractive because he functions as a kind of "artist-Hercules" in both his writing and his performing, enacting the process of "becoming" for us all. As his writing has developed, his characters have deepened, losing their tendency toward flatness and overfragmentation without losing their wit and ability to articulate what we didn't even know we felt.

He is no longer just the smart girl's heartthrob, the idol of a few clusters of theater cliques on the East and West coasts, the darling of a few discerning critics. Movie stardom and a romance with Jessica Lange pose a real danger that Shepard could fall prey to America's voracious appetite for heroes, a phenomenon he has articulated often and well:

Through bragging, a lot of early-day American heroes sprang up. Paul Bunyan, Pecos Bill, all those mythic guys emerged from fantastic "tall tales." . . . The East was intrigued and curious about all these dudes, and the West was more than willing to supply them with all the fancy embroidered "facts" of their heroism. So, even though there were real guys involved in a real environment, their deeds were largely invented to satisfy this growing hunger and intrigue from the opposite coast. That hunger never left us . . . there's still emotional space that needs filling. And it's still the same as it was then. It doesn't matter if the information on our heroes is completely made up, we still want to believe it. . . . Somebody "out there" is actually doing what cries out in us to be done. Something somehow that we know is in us, but it's not us that's doing it."[7]

Shepard knows he is a man who has his work to do, but, as Marlon Brando once commented, being a movie star is not man's work. How can the man who wrote *Angel City,* a play heavy with contempt for Los Angeles, the dream factory, feel about being the Gary Cooper of the Eighties, enjoying what *People* magazine has dubbed "the romance of the century"? He could laugh and undoubtedly does . . . sometimes, but Shepard is a complexity containing multiple points of view. From his earliest days in the New York downtown scene of the Sixties, friends were telling him he could make it big in Hollywood. He would grin, Gary Cooper fashion, mumble something, and generally slough it off. But movies and the myth of stardom had made their indelible mark on him early in life. Like the West, Shepard hasn't exactly discouraged the tall tales about himself "embroidered" by the myth-hungry East Coast.

I remember trying to imitate Burt Lancaster's smile after I saw him in *Vera Cruz.* For days I practiced in the backyard. Weaving through the tomato plants. Sneering. Grinning that grin. Sliding my upper lip up over my teeth. After a few days of practice, I tried it out on the girls at school. They didn't seem to notice. I broadened my interpretation until I started getting strange reactions from the other kids. They would look straight at my teeth and a fear would creep into their eyes. I'd forgotten how bad my teeth were. Now one of the front ones was dead and brown and overlapped the broken one right next to it. I'd actually come to believe I was in possession of perfect pearly Burt Lancaster-type teeth.[8]

A classic memory of the budding-actor genre, provoking the reader to wonder if the writer is aware that the broken, discolored teeth only serve to add a kind of James Dean rebel-boy charm to his Gary Cooper grin.

Shepard loves and despises the movies because their "tall tales" captured him early and for good. The movie house is a place of dreams, of sweet, narcotizing lies, which breed discontent and fantasy, keeping us from our real lives:

I look at the screen and I am the screen. I'm not me. I don't know who I am. I look at the movie and I am the movie. I am the star. I am the star in the movie. For days

I am the star and I'm not me. I'm me being the star. I look at my life when I come down. I look and I hate my life not being a movie. I hate my life not being a star. I hate having to eat. Having to work. Having to sleep. Having to go to the bathroom. Having to get from one place to another with no potential. Having to live in this body which isn't a star's body and all the time knowing that stars exist. That there are people doing nothing at all all their life except being in movies. Doing nothing but swimming and drinking and laughing and being driven to places full of potential. People never having to feel hot pavement or having to look at weeds growing through cracks in the city square in the eyes. People living in dreams which are the same dreams I'm dreaming but never living.[9]

In *Motel Chronicles,* Shepard describes a childhood memory: the magical transformation of a dark theater into the Africa of *King Solomon's Mines,* walking in a stupor for days afterward, to the reverberating drumbeats, in the lingering heat, colors, and smells of the jungle. No matter that he avoids interviews and publicity, lives far from any media centers, prefers to work with a community of close friends and spend the rest of his time on his Santa Fe horse ranch. Shepard belongs to the movies, and, sooner or later, he must claim his front-row seat. He may be scornful, but movies have everything that has always drawn him: the ability to create instant myths, a transient lifestyle, beautiful women, easy money, and, most of all, the power to wreak magical, alchemical transformations—to turn, for example, a dark, musty movie house in Duarte, California, into the primordial Technicolor jungles of King Solomon.

"I think there are basically two roads," Shepard told Blanche McCrary Boyd. "You either die like a dog or you die like a man. And if you die like a dog, you just go back to dust." John

Wayne himself couldn't have said it better, and Shepard really means it. His code succinctly articulates our cultural attitude of the moment, even if we all don't know just exactly what he means. But we see us in him, bigger and better than life, "the scornful pop addict," as critic John Lahr put it, seduced by America's manufactured fantasies, even transformed into one, and perhaps a little bit angry about it.

TWO

Sam Shepard Rogers the seventh was born to Sam Rogers the sixth and Jane Elaine Schook Rogers on November 5, 1943, in Fort Sheridan, Illinois, an Army base about twenty-five miles from Chicago. In keeping with family tradition, he was nicknamed Steve to distinguish him from his father: "My name came down through seven generations of men with the same name each naming the first son the same name as the father then the mothers nicknaming the sons so as not to confuse them with the fathers when hearing their names called in the open air while working side by side in the waist-high wheat."[1]

Shepard's father was in the Army Air Corps in Italy and came home soon after the war, wounded and severely disturbed: "My grandfather lost his farm," Shepard explained to *The New York Times*. "It was during the Depression and my dad was forced to join the Army so as to support his mother and younger brothers. As a kid I heard the stories and grew up knowing that my dad really suffered." Shepard's father never recovered from the "good war": an alcoholic, he wandered off from his family countless times, until his wife, tired of continually looking for him, let him be—a colorful teller of fabulous tales, living alone in the desert. Shepard loved his father, and experienced a good deal of pain for him and because of him. The specter of his father's sad fate always before him, Shepard evidently observed and absorbed the lesson well: "I'm just amazed when I catch a glimpse of who I really am. Just a little flash like the gesture of my hand in a conversation and WHAM, there's my old man. Right there, living inside me like a worm in the wood. And I ask myself, 'Where have I been all this time?' Why was I blind? Sleeping."[2]

After his two younger sisters, Deedee and Sandy, were born, the family began to migrate from base to base; this month in Rapid City, South Dakota, next in Utah, this year in Florida, and then across the country and across the Pacific to Guam, where they lived in a tin-roofed hut and Shepard's baby rattles were the bleached-out skulls of Japanese soldiers: "There were a lot of Japanese on the island who had been forced back into living in the caves and they would come down and steal clothes off the clothes-lines, and food and stuff. All the women were issued with Army Lugers, and I remember my mother shooting at them."

After Guam, his father left the Army and the family went to live in South Pasadena, California, a white, middle-class suburb, with an aunt who had some money through Mrs. Rogers's family. After the family found a house of their own, Shepard began high school, where he had "one good friend, Ernie Ernshaw—the first guy I started smoking cigarettes with. Later he joined the Navy, and I went back to see him about ten years afterwards, and he'd turned into this Hollywood slick-guy with tight pants and a big fancy hairdo. It was fantastic."[3]

Shepard's father was trying to get his degree, which had been interrupted by the Army, and was attending night school while his mother worked as a teacher: "He was very strict, my father, very aware of the need for discipline, so-called, very into studying and all that kind of stuff. I couldn't stand it—the whole thing of writing in notebooks, it was really like being jailed."[4] In later years, however, Shepard became known for his omnipresent notebook in which he made frequent notes, so much so that his playwriting class presented him with a carton full of shirt-pocket-sized writing pads.

Rogers's discipline was lightened enough to allow a little Dixieland music on the radio while he studied—and when he wasn't studying he played drums for a semiprofessional band. "That's how I learned to play," says Shepard, "just banging on his set of drums. And then I started getting better than him."[5]

The family was now living in Duarte, a few miles east of Pasadena, on an avocado ranch. Their home was a converted greenhouse, and their piece of land held livestock, horses, and chickens, as well as their avocado trees. Because of California's erratic rain supply, he and his father rigged up an irrigation system which they operated by hand every day. Shepard also made pocket money driving the little family tractor for other citrus groves in the area. Though he enjoyed agriculture and raising animals, Shepard felt wrenched away from his friends in South Pasadena: "It was a funny community, divided into three very distinct social groups. There were the very wealthy people, who had ranches up in the mountains with white-faced Hereford cattle roaming around, and swimming pools and Cadillacs. And then you'd get these very straight middle-class communities, people who sold encyclopedias and stuff like that. It was the first place where I understood what it meant to be born on the wrong side of the tracks because the railroad tracks cut right down through the middle of this place: and below the tracks were the blacks and Mexicans."[6]

Not surprisingly, young "Steve" drew to him friends as estranged and strange as he. "There was one guy who was from British Columbia—the one I wrote about in *Tooth of Crime*. He'd just come down from Canada, and he looked exactly like Elvis Presley. He had this incredible black hair-do and flash clothes, which nobody wore in school except for a few Mexicans —the white kids all wore Ivy League button-down numbers and loafers. So he was immediately ostracized, but he turned out to be a brilliant student—he didn't read any books, just got straight A grades. I got to be really good friends with him. And there were a couple of computer freaks, who were working at this aeronautics plant where they built computers for nosecones. One guy used to bring in paper bags full of amphetamine and Benzedrine from Mexico. I swear to God, those pills—if you took two of them, you were just flying. . . .

"I was thinking that I wanted to be a veterinarian, and I had a chance to actually manage a sheep ranch, but I didn't take it. I wanted to do something like that, working with animals, I even had the grand champion yearling ram at the Los Angeles County Fair one year. I did. It was a great ram."[7]

Despite his natural athletic build and prowess at the high jump, Shepard did not fulfill the image of "high school jock." He was a member of the 4-H Club, traditional locus for outsiders, even "nerds," though no one could imagine Shepard, even in the most awkward of adolescences, as a "nerd."

Shepard does not recall those high school years too fondly ("The fifties sucked dogs, man"[8]), and he preferred exploring the local foothills or playing drums to attending school.

Duarte had another favorite son—although at the time the town was unappreciative of its good fortune—one as brilliant and as out of place as was Shepard: Charles Mingus III, painter, playwright, and son of the great jazz bassist. "We didn't have any concept of a larger planet than Route 66, which was like the space program for the Fifties in California," explains Mingus. "Pasadena, Arcadia, Monrovia, Azusa, La Quinada, El Monte, San Diego—the line of towns that run from San Francisco to San Diego—the sort of circuit areas you'd go to to get away from the suburbs and sub-suburbs. Duarte is like a tail end, it was an incorporated city with the gentry from Monrovia, a sort of series of enclaves from Los Angeles, like retirement-

type people, a lot of World War II vets in the foothills screaming their guts out for morphine.

"When we were a little younger, we used to explore these
little aspects of the town, check out the back alleys, find gold
in the dentist's garbage, take it to the mineral guy, and get
stones, gems, and trade for it. A better life than public school."

Shepard and Mingus met in high school—briefly and vio-
lently—in a fistfight over a remark that faded from memory as
quickly as it had sparked tempers. Shepard graduated in 1961
and enrolled at Mount San Antonio Junior College as an agri-
cultural science major, an "aggie," still the outsider. Like any
typical California youngster, he worked summers on a horse
ranch to earn three hundred dollars for his first car, a 1932 Ford
Deuce Coupe. But he was increasingly dissatisfied and restless.

Shepard's violent fights with his father were escalating, and
though this adversity was to prove a wellspring for Shepard's
writing, at this period of his life he needed release from his
frustration and confusion:

"I hardly knew anything about the theater. I remember once
in California I went to this guy's house who was called a beatnik
by everybody at school because he had a beard and he wore
sandals. And we were listening to some jazz or something and
he sort of shuffled over to me and threw this book on my lap,
and said, 'Why don't you dig this, you know.' I started reading
this play he gave me, and it was like nothing I'd ever read before
—it was *Waiting for Godot*. And I thought, what's this guy
talking about, what is this? And I read it with a very keen
interest, but I didn't know anything about what it *was*."[9]

Shepard was inspired enough to attempt poetry and his first
play, now lost, about a girl who is raped and otherwise abused
by her father—a poor Tennessee Williams imitation, according
to its author.

Theater became an escape for Shepard. Unable to take his

father's drinking bouts and military-style discipline, Shepard auditioned for a local theater company which also traveled across the country; he saw an advertisement in the paper. They were auditioning actors for something called the Bishop's Company, so Shepard went in there and they hired him. It was through this venture that he and Mingus became friends: "I met him a second time after we graduated," Mingus recalls, "another incarnation, you might say; he was acting. Sam and I grew up on the fringes of both of the groups we were involved in. The only way I remembered him was that fistfight over some wisecrack he'd made, and we didn't become fast friends. When I saw him the second time, I didn't think about the fight, but he'd made an impression. I was eating in a diner on Route 66, like in the movie *Diner,* only everyone was black. Sam was looking around, vaguely nervous, and if I rewrote it now, I would say he was as indifferent to me as I was to him. He saw me first, came over, said, 'Hi,' something like 'We went to school together,' and asked me to be in a Bishop Company production, *Skin of Our Teeth,* at the Mission Theater, directed by a New York actress, Dorothy Chase, I think."

Mingus never rehearsed the whole piece with the entire cast. He was just doing Shepard a favor. The company needed someone black to push a boardwalk chair across the stage and Shepard had gone out and recruited Mingus for the honor. For Mingus, the experience was a revelation: "That racist grade-B mentality like *Skin of Our Teeth* never made a difference to me until I did it." When the moment came for Mingus to push a wicker chair across the stage—playing the stereotypical shuffling Tom—he rebelled wildly: "I said, 'No way, folks!' and threw the chair in the front row . . . and stood there and said, 'Fuck you, Nazis!' People were running up and down the aisles and backstage: 'Get that guy!' And I had split. The whole thing was really fascinating because nobody found me. I was on top of a phone pole looking down at everybody running around screaming, 'Kill that nigger! Where'd he go!' Sam thought it was the funniest thing he'd ever experienced. He was pretty violent, too. In fact, that's how I got to have a second opinion —my emotional reaction was really violent. The only impression I have is him cracking up, standing nearby the pole saying, 'It's a good idea to be up there.' He found me; I was panicked, freaked out, turned inside out, and he thought it was great. That kind of made me happy because then I had a handle on another view of whites that wasn't this 'Make them do what you want Robinson Crusoe–Man Friday bullshit.' It was impossible for Sam to follow the notion society put forth that white blue-eyed men were Robinson Crusoe and black men were their Fridays. We were once talking about racism and he was saying you can't do any better than the Duarte school system. It had an integrated school which was a shock to the community, so they had a trick up their sleeves, which was a separate history course. All white history classes taught white supremacy. And Sam tentatively made that statement."

It was fairly unusual at that time for a young white man and a young black man to be close friends. While they didn't get into trouble with anyone for it, "We got into trouble psychically," says Mingus. "Not the white-man's-burden trip. But here's Sam intellectually being responsible for his culture and here's me being razor sharp—not intellectually, but the words I said were cutting. He took it kind of personally, too. I mean, I'd say *you,* meaning in general, not him specifically. And he'd say, 'Whoa, slow down,' and we'd have to redefine that lots of times and deal with the emotions. Because it is his society, he did benefit from color privilege, he did get a better education, he did get a slant on things which gave him a mythology. It gave him more power to deal with matters: 'It's your right to rip mountaintops off or test atomic bombs or dig up all the gold or take all the oil or use people like objects and that's 'cause you're blond and blue-eyed.' And he'd go, '*You,* you mean *me! I* don't feel that shit!'

And I'd go, 'No, I mean *you* . . . uh, er . . . as in *one*. And by that, participating in the ethos, let's call it, of American political, cultural effect.' And he'd go, 'What in the fuck are you talking about?' And I'd try to start again.

"We were involved in a symbiotic relationship in terms of this racial stuff, in terms of what is intellectuality. The synergy of two opposites."

Though he was nearly fired after the Mingus debacle, Shepard stayed with the Bishop's Company. He and Mingus had planned to come to New York when the group went on tour, but the chair episode changed everything.

After three semesters Shepard left college and abandoned his plans to become a veterinarian for the adventure of touring with the troupe for six months, playing church communities around the country: "The religious cover was a phony. We were really a bunch of frustrated actors who couldn't find a niche," Shepard has asserted. But he enjoyed the nomadic existence, the freedom of being away from the confines and tensions of home, and he learned "what it is to make theater. We'd go into churches, mostly in New England, set up lights, do makeup, do the play, tear it down and leave to go down the road the next day." Years later, on Bob Dylan's 1977 Rolling Thunder Revue tour, the memories rushed back: "I remember this gypsy life now. It all floods back from days when I was acting in a traveling road show. Doing one-nighters on Protestant Church altars. Sleeping in strange families' empty bedrooms. Packing up and heading out again. Just the mobility of it brings the pulse of high adventure."[10]

The tour took Shepard to New York in 1963. He was nineteen years old. Charles Mingus had given up acting and was a painter, involved with that world. His father had sent for him, so he'd arrived by plane somewhat earlier and settled into a cold-water flat in a crumbling building on the Lower East Side's Avenue C. Mingus was turning a bar into a recording studio for his father: "And there was a big oak pay phone which they refused to take or even accept our offer to truck it to wherever they wanted it. I dismantled it and put it on the street—part of it was still standing. And I got inside of it and crashed it to the ground like Superman. Some asshole journalist saw it and thought, 'Oh, I'll tell this to Hedda Hopper and she'll put it in her column,' and it became a little blurb. And Sam read either that or the one that said, 'Charlie Mingus's son is working at the Village Gate as a busboy. Isn't that something? Tsk, tsk,' and he looked me up. That's how he found me."

Mingus got Shepard a job bussing tables with him at the Village Gate in Greenwich Village, a haven for all kinds of artists to find employment until they got their big break. Art d'Lugoff, who began the club in a dilapidated cellar in the biggest bum's hotel in New York City, recalls that there were times in its history that "there was more talent on the floor than on the stage." The hours were flexible, the money good, and Shepard "got to see the cream of American jazz every night for free. I worked three nights a week and got about fifty bucks a week for hardly doing anything, except cleaning up dishes and bringing Nina Simone ice, you know. It was fantastic." He also got to see great stand-up comedians such as Flip Wilson, Woody Allen, Dick Cavett, and Richard Pryor—all of whom were just beginning brilliant careers, as well as some duds from whom he learned what not to do. At one point, Mingus and Shepard considered formalizing their fun and becoming a professional comedy team, but that plan never materialized. Instead, the nights of comedy at the Gate found their way into the humor of Shepard's plays.

In the early Sixties it seemed as if every talented, disaffected youth from countries all over the world had gathered in the small community of downtown Manhattan, and Shepard had landed point blank in the center of the creative explosion: "When I arrived in New York there was this environment of art going on," Shepard later explained to the *L.A. Weekly.* "And you were right in the thing, especially on the Lower East Side. La Mama, Theater Genesis, Caffe Cino, all those theaters were just starting.

"Off-off Broadway was just to see new work done; it wasn't done as a showcase to move it somewhere else. That came later. It was all in cahoots with poetry and jazz and all that. And actors. It was kind of a phenomenon, 'cause it happened right there, in that time, and took off like a shot."

At this point, he changed his name from Steve Rogers to Sam Shepard. "My name, Samuel Shepard Rogers, was too long," he has said, "so I just dropped the *Rogers* part of it. It had been in the family for seven generations and my grandmother wasn't too happy over it." Since he could have dropped *Shepard* rather than *Rogers,* it seems a deliberate break with his heredity, an attempt to construct his own identity. According to Mingus, however, "All his life he was Steve Rogers, never any hint of an English-type name. Until the infamous midwesterner Dr. Sam Sheperd murdered his wife, in the early sixties, Sam Shepard never called himself Sam Shepard. All of a sudden, he changed his name. It was too coincidental in a way, and in a way, it was a good trigger because it was excellent publicity. The guy I knew would exploit that—he was a little sad about it, to tell the truth, but it was viable and it was humorous because people would actually go to the play to see a piece thinking 'I wonder what this guy who killed his wife and got away with it wrote?' There were people like that and that was fascinating to Sam and to me and probably to the people in the crew. And Sam was freaking out and laughing, and, at the same time, there was a profit motive involved. He was aware of box office."

Mingus recounts how the two of them played at roles, switching characters, mimicking voices of those who struck them as phony, in characters ranging from old ladies to gangsters—

telling the "truth" through their private code. He attributes their need to try on characters like suits of clothes to their mutual lack of a father's consistent and positive influence. They picked and chose from the models offered by our society, trying on "ideas" of men like "men who play women in drag," because there were so many to choose from, all the while searching for an identity that fit. "You try on this suit, this mask, this body armor," Mingus explains. It is apparent that much of Shepard's work developed from this "serious" play, from finding a character and letting it speak, an aesthetic Shepard was to later develop and present more formally to his playwriting classes.

"That's important," says Mingus, "because that's how Sam went from *acting* acting to writing. Carroll O'Connor says once he's done the Archie Bunker voice and is in character, he can write the scripts. Going from being an actor is a better activity than going from a person trying to write what they see on TV, let's say, and calling it theater, which was what most of the people around us were trying to do. Instead, you'd say something in a voice, like automatic writing, and be committed to what the actual idea was, because you'd hear yourself say this and know that it's really what's true in a dream way or true in a historical, external-to-you way, and then face that."

At first, Shepard did attempt to succeed as an actor in New York. One of his few roles was in a directors' workshop production directed by actor Don Plumley, *The Eggs of the Devil,* also known by the more titillating title, *The Secret of Father Tolentino.* Performed on March 11, 1964, written by a Filipino cook at the Rathskeller, the play is based on an incident that actually took place in the Philippines during the Japanese occupation. The central roles are a Catholic priest and his young prelate, Sacristin, which Shepard played—and well, according to Plumley: "I remember having to suggest only one little thing to him; he was very instinctive. I've never gotten to know him well because he didn't hang out much with actors. I think Shepard was into hanging out with musicians. But he was very good; he was quiet and observant. He just seemed very together for his age, which was twenty. He didn't do too much, just sort of down-home and together."

There was too much going on for Shepard to pursue work only as an actor. With the exuberant energy of kids busting out of school, Shepard and Mingus discovered the playground of New York City. They were "teammates" playing a freer, more exciting game than any they had known back West in Duarte. So they played at Eastern cowboys.

"We had a lot of good times," Mingus reports. "He's written some things that I identify as my personal experiences. I remember some events that happened that were stupid. We almost got arrested by the police for having a music concert on the roof that we thought was a neat idea. Of course, we had an old typewriter that was part of the musical instruments. It ended up with the police coming up there and making us throw off the roof one of those really ancient Smith-Corona typewriters with those big fat marshmallow-sized keys that I really wish I had now just to put a potted plant in. We were making mock poetry pieces and we had a little antenna to transmit it. It was very bizarre, but we were just having a party and some people came over and we did this goof. It was a happening about communications and stuff.

"I got him the job at the Gate and I consider it payment in full for the job he got me in *Skin of Our Teeth*. If he didn't like the job . . . he kind of used it as a theatrical thing, like we were doing a life which was like a movie, like cowboys. Our heroes were Laurel and Hardy. Sam got a letter once from Stan Laurel —that's my memory—and he was living in a trailer camp. It was really a pisser. Here's this old guy who did so much great stuff and he died in obscurity. It was really touching to see the respect Sam deeply felt for the talent of people who went before. He felt deeply about a lot of stuff and frustration about things that couldn't be changed. But you can't imagine what the world is like if your heroes are Laurel and Hardy. There's a grace and stupidity and naturalness, and the possibility of being a genius like they were, based on really studying them. We looked at all the movies, over and over. We laughed—it was a lot of fun.

"At the Gate, the announcer also managed us, and she would do white glove tests. It was very precise, like lining up for reveille, and Sam felt rebellious against that, put upon by standards no one else noticed or needed to maintain. We were constantly supposed to be on the alert to be available. I'll put it this way: What I had to say about the chair in *Skin of Our Teeth,* he had to say about class distinctions, artificial assumptions of anglicizing everything, and a dude with a cane, a tweed suit with jodhpurs and vest and cap, sitting there as royal as you please, besotted if not totally oblivious to Sam, and a pawn in that game."

Somehow, Shepard managed to send his bus tray loaded with plates and glasses in a perfect arc right into that pompous man's lap. But, as Mingus explains, "Sam was compelled. It was like the fly on the nose. It was *right in the moment;* if Sam hadn't done it, he would have died. It was compelling, necessary, and it caused waves. I think he was admonished, and I think other things led to his leaving. He was fired, yes. There were a lot of people who were hypocritical, but that dude was everything at once. He manifested it all. Sam didn't care about the outcome. I apologized—Sam was reckless."

Years later, Shepard wrote a more literary version of the incident in a piece reminiscing about the nights at the Gate: "I knocked over a candle once while [Nina Simone] was singing. . . . The hot wax spilled all over a businessman's suit. I was called into the manager's office. The businessman was standing there with this long splash of hardened wax down his pants. It looked like he'd come all over himself. I was fired that night."[11]

In the background of Mingus and Shepard's play, a new

culture was taking root: R. D. Laing was singing the praises of being schizophrenic, saying that the rent in consciousness was the natural psychic state of modern man. Shepard, and quite a few others, took this notion and ran with it. Diane Arbus was photographing freaks, making objects of art out of society's debris. Lenny Bruce was being hilarious and too telling . . . and getting arrested for it at the Village Vanguard. At the Five Spot, Ornette Coleman and Charles Mingus were redefining jazz. And a new form of American theater was forming. Joe Cino started the Caffe Cino in 1959, quickly followed by the Judson Poets' Theater, and Ellen Stewart's Cafe La Mama officially raised its curtain on June 28, 1963. Run on shoestring budgets, these theaters were labors of love for everyone involved. With the founding of Theater Genesis at St. Mark's-in-the-Bouwerie, church funds became available, and gradually, slowly, private donations and grants became available. In their wonderful *The Off Off Broadway Book,* Albert Poland and Bruce Mailman tell how it all began and what it was about:

> Three charismatic personalities, Joe Cino, Al Carmines, and Ellen Stewart, created the theatres and kept them alive. These theatres, although individual, had a similar aesthetic. . . .
>
> The plays of Off Off have a common language that is built on a set of new symbols. The new symbols are a function of the new audience, for Off Off is an audience-oriented theatre. Not since the great age of the American music hall and the melodrama has there been such real audience devotion and interaction. The audience participates; they boo, they cheer, but most of all they *enjoy* the plays and they attend the theatre because the new symbols are as familiar to them as they are to the playwrights. One need only be familiar with general American sociology to

understand the new syntax: the movies on Saturday nights, popcorn, Cokes, the radio, TV, comic strips, drugs, etc.

Unlike earlier artists of this century who broke new ground, these writers do not have to invent or revitalize myths to mine their symbols. Yeats, for example, had to reestablish the whole of Irish mythology to draw adequately powerful symbols for his poetry. . . .

The playwrights of Off Off have their mythology at hand—American folk art.[12]

American folk art is expressed in our movies, TV, pop music, and fashion. The attitude of the time grew out of a camp attitude toward contemporary culture—a broad wink of complicity between performers and a select, understanding audience, who felt privileged to sit in uncomfortable folding chairs in shabby basements, because these zero-budget productions were new and special, something just beginning.

The new form evolved because of its economic limitations, a theatre that was bone-clean, depending on the very vigor of the production to make it work. The result is a new acting and directing style. Transitions are not made in a logical way. Explication and similar devices are no longer necessary. Using impressionism, expressionism, Brecht's alienation theories in combination with Artaud's horrors, they produced a rich collage that brought a new strength to their drama. It was not planned. It was what evolved. Did Cino, Judson, and La Mama invent the styles of this theatre or were the styles the result of the limitation? There are no answers to these questions. There was a fusion and this fusion created a body of work.[13]

In the midst of this cultural ferment and theatrical revolution, young, lean Sam Shepard, urban cowboy, leaned up against a wall, folded his arms, and watched. He was beginning to realize that he didn't have to write about people and places out of a secondhand Tennessee Williams fantasy. He could take his own life—in Guam, in Duarte, his problems with his father, his adventures loping through the canyons of Manhattan with his "pardner" Charles—place these experiences against a backdrop of the symbols of American "kulture," and transform them any way his imagination wanted into theater, into something that would take on a new life separated, cleansed, and differentiated from ordinary existence. He was beginning to understand the alchemical magic of making theater, of creating a transcendent experience he could share with understanding others, his *real* family.

Mingus recalls the time he and Shepard visited the Cherry Lane, an off-Broadway house, to see some of Edward Albee's one-act plays: "They had very bizarre talking heads kinds of elements: like two Ping-Pong balls, one character on each side of the stage with a follow spot sort of bouncing back and forth. These were very abstract things which, like the work of Beckett, Pinter, and Ionesco, made a strong impression, I'm sure, on his work. I saw elements of that kind of ambiguity and that sort of cinematography in his work. And it was the goal to make it more real, not believable, because everything is believable. I think that was the goal Joe Chaikin was pursuing: the no-play concept. The lights are on, you don't see a curtain—you don't have to—it's about you experiencing what you believe, and it's about people pursuing the pleasure of being correct rather than the effect of affecting an audience, making them cry, making them laugh."

Ralph Cook, a former actor, salesman, and teacher, was also working at the Gate with Shepard and Mingus. It was he who founded Theater Genesis in 1964 to "discover authentic theatre voices and develop them toward a kind of subjective realism." Cook was looking for writers who were "working things out in themselves through their writing. . . . Worthwhile things could come from a radical nature trying to find itself in society."

Trading emotion for energy, the audiences were not dealt their accustomed allotment of sentiment and catharsis: "Often they were made to *live.* "[14] The new theater subverted the classic theatrical axiom "to hold a mirror up to nature." As Murray Mednick, playwright-director and close friend of Shepard, put it, "What is happening onstage is not a mirror, it's what's happening."

In the midst of what was happening Shepard was "the one to watch," as canny Ellen Stewart told everyone. He had the gifts but he was also in the right place at the right time— working at the Gate during a period when a dynamic new aesthetic was emerging, inspired by the jazz, talking theater with his co-workers—Mingus, Cook, Kevin O'Connor, Robert Lyons, and others, all special talents as well.

"I was very lucky to have arrived in New York at that time, though," acknowledged Shepard, "because the whole off-off-Broadway theatre was just starting—like Ellen Stewart with her little café, and Joe Cino, and the Judson Poets' Theatre and all these places. It was just a lucky accident really that I arrived at the same time as that was all starting. This was before they had all become famous, of course—like Ellen just had this little loft, served hot chocolate and coffee, did these plays. On the lower East Side there *was* a special sort of culture developing. You were so close to the people who were going to the plays, there was really no difference between you and them—your own experience was their experience, so that you began to develop that consciousness of what was happening. . . . I mean nobody knew what was happening, but there was a sense that something was going on. People were arriving from Texas and

Arkansas in the middle of New York City, and a community was being established. It was a very exciting time."[15]

One can fantasize a somewhat more sophisticated version of a scene from a Mickey Rooney–Judy Garland movie happening one night at the Gate: "Hey gang, let's make a play!" However it did happen, Theater Genesis's second production was a double bill of Sam Shepard's one-act plays *Cowboys* and *Rock Garden*.

THREE

"**C**owboys are really interesting to me," Shepard said, "these guys, most of them really young, about sixteen or seventeen, who decided they didn't want anything to do with the East Coast, with that way of life, and took on this immense country, and didn't have any real rules. Just moving cattle, from Texas to Kansas City, from the North to the South, or wherever it was.

"I wrote the original *Cowboys,* and then I rewrote it and called it *#2,* that's all. The original is lost now—but, anyway, it got done at St. Mark's. And that just happened because Charles and me used to run around the streets playing cowboys in New York. We'd both had the experience of growing up in California, in that special kind of environment, and between the two of us there was a kind of camaraderie, in the midst of all these people who were going to work and riding the buses. In about 1963, anyway—five years or so later it all suddenly broke down."[1]

But before it all broke down for Shepard and he left New York, first for England and later for the West Coast, he and Mingus reveled in what Norman Mailer has described as "the Wild West of American Nightlife." *Cowboys* described in a somewhat Brechtian fashion Mingus and Shepard's rousting around Manhattan like "doggies" on the plain. *Rock Garden* is a piece of deadpan slapstick, the last scene of which was picked up for inclusion in the multiauthored sex revue *Oh, Calcutta!* directed by Jacques Levy and produced by Hilly Elkins.

"*Rock Garden* is about leaving my mom and dad," said Shepard. "It happens in two scenes. In the first scene the mother is lying in bed ill while the son is sitting in a chair, and she is talking about this special sort of cookie that she makes, which is marshmallow on salt crackers melted under the oven. It's called Angels on Horseback, and she has a monologue about it. And then the father arrives in the second scene. The boy doesn't say anything, he's just sitting in this chair, and the father starts to talk about painting the fence around the house, and there's a monologue about that in the course of which the boy keeps dropping asleep and falling off his chair. Finally, the boy has a monologue about orgasm that goes on for a couple of pages and ends in him coming all over the place, and then the father falls off the chair. The father also talks about this rock garden, which is his obsession, a garden where he collects all these rocks from different sojourns to the desert."[2]

Kevin O'Connor starred in both plays: "It all came out of his working at the Village Gate. I helped Ralph start the theater. Ralph and I were waiters, Charles and Sam were busboys. Stephanie Gordon was the daughter of the manager of the club and Bobby Lyons was a waiter. I don't know where Lee Kissman came from. We did that show at a great loss—our best nights at the Gate were Friday and Saturday nights, which we gave up to perform for no money."

For *Cowboys,* there were no painted scrims and flats. Shepard and Mingus created a total environment: Sand and gravel covered the floor, lights blinked from sawhorses, and a stereo blasted the car sounds of a night street, collected during a trip out to New Jersey with a Wollensack tape recorder.

"We were by the turnpike at a roadside Presbyterian or Methodist church with gravel in front," Mingus recalls, "driving around their circular driveway in a car or truck—I don't remember which—tape-recording the sound of the gravel with a microphone with no lights, just the light from the church's façade. Then we were on the highway crouching down with microphones, panning at trucks as they went by, and getting really excited. 'Oh, there's a good one!' Some highway patrol–type cops see this, and it's like eleven o'clock at night. And we don't have permission, nobody went to get authority to do this, so they drove us out of town. They put us on the borderline. They had no idea what we were doing. They thought we were like Martians. They didn't know what one would do with a tape recorder for a piece of theater in New York City."

Their peers understood after *Cowboys* premiered. "Everyone got wild—they were on the same wavelength," recalls Mingus. But the mainstream critics seemed to have the understanding of New Jersey cops: uninterested and unaware of the innovative, bold new theater exploding just a few blocks away from their off-Broadway beats. When they did make their way to Genesis's new offering, they dismissed Shepard's work as a bad imitation of Beckett. "Jerry Talmer from the *New York Post* came," recalled Shepard in an interview with *The New York Times,* "and all these guys said it was a bunch of shit, imitated Beckett or something like that. I was ready to pack it in and go back to California."

Shepard might have slunk all the way home to anonymity but for the visit to Genesis one night of two young men: Bill Hart, writer, director, and presently literary manager at New York's Public Theater, and Michael Smith, playwright, musician, and theater critic for the *Village Voice*. At the time, Smith was a specialist, the *only* one, in the emerging downtown theater scene. Bill Hart recalls the experience:

"The first time I ever saw a play of Shepard's, I went with Michael Smith, who reviewed it. We were friends and totally unexpecting: We had gone to see Lee Kissman in it, who was a friend of mine and had been telling me about this really interesting writer. I was simply astonished by it because it was like he was a bop playwright. It was like that spontaneous prosody of Ginsberg, Kerouac—what they were to poetry and the novel. And there were absolute connections to music. Sam talks about how the voice has to hit the air. It was the sound of the day and there was also astonishing formalness to it. It had the credibility of a dream. He always talks about how he has trouble with ending a play. That's because he's going for a struggle so complex that it's unresolvable: There are so many elements, many of them hidden. His plays were done very well right at the beginning, because the acting that was going on then was right, what was coming out of Genesis was not like Actors Studio people. They were off the streets and really connected with music and a lot of physical acting, so they knew what they were doing.

"I stayed up all night, just going over with Michael how meaningful this all was. I couldn't shut up about it and I remember Lee Kissman needed some clothes and Michael gave him a whole bunch of stuff. It was a real celebratory feeling. I felt elated: He had literally altered my consciousness, which is the greatest thing a piece of theater can do, make you feel a totally different way which you didn't even know. It worked like rhythm and blues, like jazz, like Ginsberg, but he was a whole new thing. Then Michael wrote this great review in the *Voice,* saying a new playwright is born; a strange thing to say, but absolutely right. And then, from the earliest day, everybody thought of Shepard as the best—right away."

Michael Smith was equally struck: "I'd been specializing in reviewing little theaters, which were just starting to exist, for two or three years. There'd begun to be a few little cafés like Take 3, Phase 2, and they also did plays at the Figaro. The Cino was going and La Mama had done a few things in basements. It was still very scattered.

"I went to Shepard's plays—I couldn't figure out for a while what it was about, those plays of Sam's that seemed so amazing and unlike anything I'd ever seen before. I decided after a while that it had to do with their showing a state of mind that I only knew by getting high and smoking pot, which was something I had only recently started doing, and it had changed my consciousness. Suddenly, there it was in a play. It really wasn't only Sam who was responsible for that.

"But it somehow came from him—something so free and direct about those plays. They seemed to catch the actual movement of the minds of people I knew. It was something I had never seen before. A little bit similar to what was happening in popular music—Dylan, for example, who seemed to be singing about what he himself felt and experienced, rather than some preestablished range of feelings. He [Shepard] seemed to be able to take chances and be very fast and free with his fantasy when he wrote. Years later, I once tried to write a play with him in collaboration on his farm in Nova Scotia. He was freer. I got all hung up in trying to figure it out and think it through and puzzle it out, and got left behind in the dust. It was very frustrating. It didn't matter to him.

"Maybe it was just my attitude, but it seemed to me that there was a very nonexploitative attitude behind all the work then; there was no sense that people were laying the groundwork for a career or looking for worldly success. The work was done for the moment, for its own sake. Sam's work too. There was no sense it was being done to add up to anything. In hindsight, it's easy to see how it led up to his present success, but I don't think there was that attitude at all.

"The critics were missing everything at that point. None of them were picking up on the fact that there was a whole wave of new stuff about to happen and it was important to be on your toes and watch for it. I'm sure my review gave a real shot in the arm to Theater Genesis. I don't remember what I wrote. I'm sure it was a rave review. I loved the work and I tried to share my enthusiasm. The *Village Voice* was a key theater paper at that point, so people just flocked to those plays."

Only twenty years old, Shepard responded to his success by working even harder. He began turning out one-act pieces at a furious pace. "There was nothing else to do," he said in a *New York Times* interview. "I didn't really have any references for the theater, except for the few plays I'd acted in. But in a way I think that was better for me, because I didn't have any idea about how to shape an action into what is seen—so the so-called originality of the early work just comes from ignorance. I just didn't know."

His work shared many elements with that of his peers: heavy use of sound and music, avoidance of the classical unities, a pop sensibility, lack of sentiment, and a challenge to the audience to really experience what was immediately there. At the same time, all the peculiarly Shepardesque notes were sounded right from the beginning: Music, the art form that gives purest expression to the ineffable qualities of spirit and emotion, did more than support—it vibrated through the words and actions of his characters, just as the "cream of jazz" informed and overlapped Shepard's endless talks about the new theater with his Gate co-workers Mingus, Cook, O'Connor, and Lyons. Also, then as now, Shepard was almost helplessly fascinated with the process of his own character, although not to the point of narcissism. He burrows into its deepest recesses, restructuring and transforming his experience until it defines not just himself, but a world. We see us in him—his vision resonates in us, and ultimately, that is what makes all the difference. And from the beginning, his instinctive sense of form seemed to flow, as do his athletic and musical talents, from a natural sense of rhythm and balance. In those days, he wrote at amazing speed, never changing a word.

Instinctively a private person, it was as hard for Shepard to have his work performed in public as it had been for him to act in front of an audience and be reviewed in a public press: "It was frightening at first. I can remember defending myself against it mostly. I was really young for one thing, about nineteen, and I was very uptight about making a public thing out of something you do privately. And I was strongly influenced by Charles—he was very into not selling out, and keeping himself within his own sphere of reference. I felt that by having the play become public, it was almost like giving it away or something. I was really hard to get along with in those days, actually. I would always bitch a lot during rehearsals and break things up.

"It changes everything, you know, from being something that you do in quite a private way to something you do publicly. Because no matter how much you don't like the critics, or you don't want them to pass judgement on what you're doing, the fact that they're there reflects the fact that a play's being done in public. It means that you steadily become aware of people going to see your plays—of audiences. Not just critics, but people."[3]

Nineteen sixty-five was the first of many busy years for Shepard: *Dog* and *Rocking Chair,* two one-acters, or "vibrations" as poet Michael McClure called them, opened at La Mama on February 10. They remain unpublished and obscure, and rightly so, according to their author: "*Dog* was about a black guy—which later I found out was uncool for a white to write about in America. It was about a black guy on a park bench, a sort of *Zoo Story*-type play. I don't even remember *Rocking Chair,* except it was about somebody in a rocking chair."[4]

Shepard admired Edward Albee, author of *Zoo Story.* He discovered Albee's Greenwich Village address, rang his doorbell, and presented him with a suitcase full of plays. Albee read them and selected one, *Up to Thursday,* about a boy facing the draft, for inclusion in the New Playwrights Series of February

1965 at the Cherry Lane Theater. On the same bill with Shepard's play were early works by Lanford Wilson and Paul Foster. Once again Shepard was dipping into his own life for his subject: He had avoided the draft that year by pretending to be a heroin addict. Shepard later dismissed the play as "a bad exercise in absurdity, I guess. This kid is sleeping in an American flag, he's only wearing a jockstrap or something, and there's four people on stage who keep shifting their legs and talking. I can't remember it very well—it's only been done once. It was a terrible play, really. It was the first commercial production I'd done, and it was put on with a bunch of other plays, in the off-off-Broadway-moves-off-Broadway kind of bill."[5] But Albee championed his young protégé, noting in a *Village Voice* review of *Icarus's Mother,* a production that opened later that year, that "what Shepard's plays are about is a great deal less interesting than how they are about it."

During the casting of *Up to Thursday,* Shepard was still sharing Mingus's place on Avenue C, where they paid a ridiculously low rent because the building was near collapse. Young, pretty, red-haired Joyce Aaron came to audition for a role. "In the audition, I had to laugh and laugh without stopping," she recalls. "It was part of the role. I was laughing, hysterical, and then I heard this giggle from the back of the theater. It was Sam. I did *Up to Thursday* at the Cherry Lane Theater with Kevin O'Connor, Robert F. Lyons, Stephanie Gordon, and Harvey Keitel. Sam and I began to live with each other, sharing our lives and our work."

Joyce had to go to Chicago to perform *The Knack,* and Shepard arrived when the play opened. He wrote his play *Chicago* from that experience. The girl is called Joy, she bakes cookies for her man, just as Joyce did in preparation for Sam's visit, ignoring the pleas of her neighbors, Gerome Ragni and Jim Rado, to help them improvise and write this piece they called *Hair.*

On April 16, 1965, *Chicago,* featuring Kevin O'Connor as the disaffected young man who sits in a bathtub throughout the play, opened on a double bill with Lawrence Ferlinghetti's *The Customs Inspector in Baggy Pants.* The play opens to the tattoo of a policeman's nightstick while someone recites the Gettysburg Address. The curtain then rises on Stu sitting in a tub, splashing water. His girl, Joy, calls out that the cookies are ready, and Stu stands up, revealing wet pants and sneakers. Joy brings him a towel, but he wraps it around his neck and Joy then gets into the tub with him. A friend, Myra, comes in, watches them, then tells Joy to pack. Some more friends, Sally and Jim, come in carrying fishing rods and suitcases, talking and eating biscuits. Stu periodically lapses into conversations with an imaginary fish named Joe and talks to Joy in an old woman's voice. Joy exits, then returns, pulling a wagonload of suitcases. Everyone says good-bye and then, with the exception of Stu, sits facing the audience. The play ends on Stu's monologue describing the experience of a creature emerging from the water to breathe air. The stage set was bare but for a bathtub.

O'Connor, who played Stu, recalls that "Sam would come to rehearsals because he dug seeing the thing happen. He was wonderful because he'd laugh at his own stuff—he'd get a kick out of it if something was really happening. He'd enjoy it and fall off the chair. It was really a nice experience.

"We were on a roll with Shepard," continues O'Connor. "He acted in *Up to Thursday* when Bobby Lyons got hurt. He was hit badly by a cop's nightstick and Sam went on for him. He was very good. We were acting a whole idea of Sam's about America at that time. During that period, he was with Joyce, of course, and out of a personal experience of hers when she went for a job, he wrote *Chicago,* which I also performed in. It was basically me in a bathtub. The bathtub came from Sam and Charles's apartment—we walked it over to St. Mark's from Avenue C. There was a lot of that kind of thing done in those days. It's exactly twenty years ago, and the bathtub is still sitting in the basement of La Mama—Ellen Stewart just showed it to me. He wrote that play very fast and I did it all over the world."

Shepard says he wrote *Chicago* in one day: "The stuff would just come out, and I wasn't really trying to shape it or make it into any big thing. I would have a picture and just start from there. A picture of a guy in a bathtub, or of two guys on stage with a sign blinking—you know, things like that. . . .

"When you talk about images, an image can be seen without looking at anything—you can see something in your head, or you can see something on stage, or you can see things that don't appear on stage, you know. The fantastic thing about theatre is that it can make something be seen that's invisible, and that's where my interest in theatre is—that you can be watching this thing happening with actors and costumes and light and set and language, and even plot, and something emerges from beyond that, and that's the image part that I'm looking for, that's the sort of added dimension."[6]

Most actors had difficulty in understanding exactly how the "invisible was seen"—how to find the inner meaning underlying the apparent chaos—in Shepard's early plays. O'Connor says he would read but not understand the plays: "I did them because they were an opportunity to do something, and there were those long speeches which were a lot of fun. There were kind of special relationships built. When I did *Cowboys,* I didn't understand it at all, but I knew there was a very special relationship, and we figured it out—Bobby and I—that we were doing it for each other. It was kind of on the edge of an improvisation without being an improvisation, and it was written out of Charles Mingus and [Sam] playing games around New York City. Sam intuitively had a kind of theatrical sense that one didn't get from reading a thing, but when you did it, it was funny, it was new. The main thing is you were in a world. He

40 ———

taught me that you have to create a world there and Sam did. If you got into that world, people would hook into it, and it would come out theatrically, and you were having a real experience doing it. In some of his early plays there was a kind of vaudevillian edge that Sam had. Most of his plays were meant to take place on a proscenium—he writes for that—or a space in front of you. He sees things coming on from the side and going off from the side—that's part of the world he's creating.

"Sam's original use of language was also something one couldn't get from just reading it because it would look like some instruction about something or a list of facts. You'd ask 'Why is this here?' and then you'd figure out what the subtext of all that was—the monologues and stories he would break into. The language was very original because it wasn't political in the overt sense. It was like facts and figures—sometimes like off the back of a matchbook cover—but it was put together in such a way that it was really striking and compelling. But you couldn't tell that without doing it and finding a way to do it."

According to O'Connor, Shepard was fortunate in his association with Ralph Cook, the founder and leading director of Theater Genesis, who knew how to direct his plays—he'd found a way to penetrate and realize Shepard's unique vision and style. "Ralph found a kind of way of letting Sam speak for himself," O'Connor says. "What he had put in originally was where it would go, and Ralph found actors who could invest it with themselves so it made a real connection. And we were all a community, which helped a lot. Ralph wouldn't impose. He would try to figure out what's going on. He knew you had to be coming from something real. But, at the same time, I had the experience of being directed by Ralph in *Chicago* at Genesis originally and then by Tom O'Horgan redoing it for the La Mama touring group. I had that experience a couple of times. It was fine because the homework had already been done and Tom could make a better show. So I see a balance there, and

I think Sam in his own direction understands it, too. You have to be coming from something that's in the text, and, at the same time, you have to make it more than real. There's a kind of theatrical reality Sam is going for."

Michael Smith shares O'Connor's opinion that Ralph Cook was essential to Shepard's early work: "For a long time I thought Ralph was the only director who did his work right, made it live the way it wanted to without superimposing something on it. I've seen a lot of productions of Sam's work which really didn't work. You could see that the play was there, buried under all sorts of things extraneous to it. Ralph was so direct in the way he worked with the actors and Sam. He seems like a very important person in the early definition of Sam's work."

Smith was not as generous in the self-review of his own direction of a Shepard play, *Icarus's Mother,* in an article he published in the *Village Voice.* The play concerns five young people on a Fourth of July picnic who are lying on their backs watching an airplane circle overhead while they wait for the fireworks display to begin. The discussion gets more and more technical. One man, Frank, goes off for a walk while the two women go off in another direction. Howard and Bill play around with the barbecue and a blanket, sending up smoke signals. Frank returns and the two men convince him that the women went to find him to tell him a secret. The women return, telling how the plane buzzed low overhead as they squatted in the bushes, peeing. Howard and Bill tell the women that Frank reported the plane crashed, and the women race off to see the wreckage. Frank then returns with the story that the plane actually did crash, which he describes graphically against the background of the fireworks display. The other two men become more and more hysterical. When Pat and Jill return from the plane-crash site, Howard and Bill are clutching each other's hands and warning everyone away from their picnic area.

The play is clearly a challenge to the abilities of even the most imaginative veteran director, but Michael Smith made few excuses for himself. In an open, forthright, and eminently instructive analysis of his mistakes, Smith notes that though he corrected some of his errors during the final stages of rehearsals, "the production retained the scars of my early mistakes." In a recent conversation, Smith recalled that though Shepard was present at rehearsals, it was difficult for Smith to direct the play: "The whole communication between me and the cast and Shepard was very difficult in that play. It was hard to get that play right. One of the things was it was technically difficult: It had a campfire right in the middle of the stage from which they were to send smoke signals with a blanket. To do that in the Caffe Cino, which was a tiny low-ceilinged room, without asphyxiating everyone, was near impossible. Also, I couldn't get from Sam what it was he really had in mind, what he wanted done. He had just written it and expected it to happen. It's a perfectly reasonable way for a playwright to work if he doesn't have to direct his own work, but I'm sure he's learned since then, now that he directs his own plays.

"Later he gave me *Geography of a Horse Dreamer*—that play has people blasted away with shotguns, and I looked at that and said, 'Good Lord, how in the world am I supposed to do this on a stage?' I had asked him for a play to direct and he'd given me that one, but I never did do it.

"The other thing about *Icarus* is I didn't deal with the naturalistic acting problems in the play. I was dealing with the symbolism of the play in my work with the actors, rather than dealing with the fact that they were on a picnic. You can't play symbolism—you have to play the reality and the symbolism works from its own accord. I just didn't know how to help the actors. I was a very inexperienced director and the play was difficult for actors. The actor who had a big monologue at the end had a terrible time with it. It was a psychological problem and I didn't know how to help. He couldn't even get his breath out to be heard and finally had to clasp his hands across his diaphragm to increase his breath pressure, pushing his voice out. That's a pretty desperate measure for an actor who had a perfectly good voice. Sam was very inarticulate about how to help, unable to explain. He had perfectly good intentions, but was unable to explain anything more than what he'd written or tell what things specifically meant.

"There was no conscious career intention behind his work and the meaning of the work was never defended. It was somehow important not to bring it up. It was uncool. Somehow as soon as the meaning of a work was brought up, the work would somehow dissolve, and it was going to slip away. You were undermining the ability of a person to function if anything too specific was said about anything. I had that feeling for a long time and it was true of a lot of Sam's early work, that it was very unclear about what's happening. To say that the plays don't mean—they do—is a kind of cop-out. It was a style of the time not to be able to be direct about content. I don't mean it's better to be rational or obvious, but it sort of went on various levels at the same time and it made it very hard for the actors to figure out what they were doing."

Shepard's later work has grown increasingly accessible without becoming obvious. He has also acquired the practice of rewriting—up to thirteen drafts before the final version of *True West*—but for most of his early career, Shepard hated to rewrite, disdaining reconsideration of his work as antithetical to his credo of "action writing," which was inspired by painter Jackson Pollock's method of "action painting." And, as Smith surmised, Shepard's later experience directing his own work was instructive. "I've found I'm too flippant about what I write," Shepard later decided. "It's too easy to dash something off and say, okay, now act it; because when it comes down to the flesh-and-blood thing of making it work, it's a different world. I think that's where the rewriting comes in—if it seems that the angle that the actor has to come at is too impossible or too difficult."[7]

Though Shepard was often disappointed with productions of his plays—sometimes he was almost jealously protective—he never responded by endlessly reworking any single play. Instead, each play stimulated him to move forward in a progression, toward something built on what he had absorbed from the experience of the last production: "I find it hard to remain with a certain attachment to things that I wrote. I've heard that a lot of writers make reams of notes before they even go into the thing, but with me I write the plays before I get to another kind of play, and each play may be a sort of evolution to something else. I always feel like leaving behind rather than hanging on to them."[8]

Perhaps no one understood his genius and promoted Shepard as enthusiastically in the early days as did Joyce Aaron. He lived with her, and she watched him transform their life together into his plays, in which she also performed. Aaron introduced Shepard to Joe Chaikin and to Jacques Levy, both directing at the Open Theater, and to Wynn Handman, founder of the American Place Theater—initiating relationships that were to prove extremely fruitful for everyone concerned. Shepard had written *Chicago* when Joyce was performing in that city; *Red Cross* came out of another job she had, playing at Philadelphia in the Park and living in a cabin; *La Turista* grew out of their experiences traveling through Mexico, while Shepard was writing furiously, on broken-down buses, in little fleabag hotels.

It was during their harrowing plane ride through a storm that Shepard swore he'd never board a plane again—a vow he's kept to this day. Aaron recalls that on their return, "we went back to Mexico City and he said, 'I'm not taking an airplane.' And I said, 'What are we going to do?' We had sixty-five dollars and we took a bus from Mexico City to New York City. I think it took four or five days."

Aaron didn't perform in *Icarus's Mother* because she and Shepard had taken acid: "I was really disturbed, so I decided I didn't want to act in that play." Her description of that experience is particularly interesting not only in its revelation of Shepard's caring aspect, but in its illustration of how he took the raw material of his life—in this case, of *their* life—and reshaped it into a literary experience. In *Motel Chronicles* there's a long piece relating Shepard's visit to a red-haired woman. Their relationship is ending. He feels her presence in the room "mourning somewhere." She freaks out, becomes semicatatonic and incapable of speech, suddenly pulls out of it, dials her mother's telephone number, and brightly announces she's coming home for a little visit.

In actuality, the piece is based on Joyce Aaron's acid experience, which happened long before she and Sam parted, when "Sam sort of pulled me through this amazing trip. When I read his *Motel Chronicles,* the story of the redheaded woman sitting on a bed, brokenhearted because he leaves, I realized the whole story was around this acid trip and he transplanted it into this home scene. He took the parting that we had and the acid experience and wove them together. It was interesting how he did that because it was probably in his memory that way. The truth is we were together when I had this acid trip and I couldn't speak—I think it's in the book. I was stuttering: 'Duk, duk, duk.' It was a very strong experience for both of us. He really pulled me through. He nursed me, gave me milk in a bottle and nursed me back into language. I was writing notes —I have them somewhere. I wrote, "I am in the . . .' and then I drew a little water sac, a little fetus in a water bag, so he knew where I was. And then I wrote, 'I don't like' —somebody had walked into the room— 'he is big like a big tree.' Then I wrote,

'I am a wo-man.' It was really incredible. He knew a lot; he helped me go through the experience of my own birth. If it wasn't for him, I think I would have been hospitalized. It was really tough and we were staying with people while we were doing his play *Fourteen Hundred Thousand* in Minnesota."

An artist herself, Aaron understood well that though she was with Sam Shepard the man, she was also with Sam Shepard the observer and transformer, and that all her experience with him was subject to his study, his elucidation of the "many, many possibilities [that] could be going on." In her essay "Clues in a Memory," Aaron wrote:

> Perhaps because we were close during that period, I never knew where our life—where *my* life—was going to turn up on the page, or later on some stage, but inevitably there was always some aspect of our experience together that I would recognize. Yet I never felt exposed by Sam—he transformed whatever he drew on. I watched him write. I traveled with him. I knew where his plays came from, what their sources were. I saw how and when he didn't rewrite, and how and when he did. I read the plays out loud to him.

Aaron understood Shepard's vision from the very beginning:

> Sam is a recorder of the authentic voice. He starts from a certain perception of daily life, and then transforms that into a specific voice—a voice with its own rhythms and shifting consciousness, its unique, particular curve or leap. You can track that leap by following the flow of his language. Each voice is different, and speaks from a different place inside you. That is part of the theatrical challenge and wonder of speaking Sam's language.[9]

"I had a very good time with him," she recalls in conversation. "We had a very good working relationship." She wrote:

> You can't approach Sam's plays according to the usual acting terms and conditions—there are no rules, because he has broken them. . . . It is a mistake to play the poetry in Sam's plays. What you are doing then becomes precious, and so does the play—you are describing a state rather than embodying it. If you don't enact the moment that Sam creates, you will miss it—and it won't come back again. Unless you make the leap, you're lost.
>
> You make the leap through the imagination. You could compare it to jamming, or improvising on a single note. Or even having a baby. When you're having a baby, you push. Nobody tells you how to push, or when—there's just a certain moment when your whole body says: "Push." Giving birth to one of Sam's monologues is similar. . . . [10]

Shepard had "deep knowledge, he knew what he was doing," asserts Aaron. "He always wrote by longhand, sitting in a corner, hours at a time, with a hand going through his hair. That was a gesture I remember about him because it was a constant gesture. I can still see him. He was really consumed. He talked a lot to me about what he was writing. He was very concentrated in longhand and very rarely rewrote in those days, except *La Turista*. We were in rehearsal for *La Turista* and he just threw out one act and brought in another. He changed the whole second act.

"He had a wonderful sense of humor, he was quiet—he's a very complex person. He could be moody, he could be very funny, he could be very giggly, very thoughtful, sometimes very paranoid—a very sensitive guy.

"I predicted he would be a movie star way back then. I said,

'Sam, you know, you belong in the movies. You could be one of those Gary Cooper types.' He said, 'Yeah, well . . .' When they found him or he found them—I don't know how it happened—I just laughed because I had predicted it. I think he has a great persona on film." In her essay, Aaron noted:

Sam himself—his presence and instinct—was usually the most illuminating element whenever I worked on his plays. I always sensed that he knew his material better than anyone else and that he could probably *act* it better than anyone else, that he really knew what he wanted to happen on the stage—in the theatre—even though in those early days, he was hardly aware of the actor's technique and vocabulary.[11]

Jacques Levy, one of the most innovative directors to emerge from the off-off-Broadway movement, recalls that he met Shepard at Aaron's urging: " 'I know this writer—you're going to love this writer.' She used to say that to a lot of people. She was really crazy about his stuff and she was right. She's a smart girl." Aaron brought Shepard to the Open Theater, where Levy and he met. "I was one of the regular directors," Levy says, "although I had just started and was going down to the sessions on a regular basis. Joe Chaikin was there. Joyce was one of the actresses and we got along very well. We were like members of a Jewish family. She was very important to Sam at the beginning, she really was, all the female characters were based on her.

"Sam and I struck it off really well, and I did *Red Cross* when it was done off-Broadway—his first off-Broadway play—on a double bill with a John Guare play at the Provincetown Playhouse. I did *Red Cross* twice: The first time was at Judson Church, and it was the first time I worked with Sam."

Unlike Michael Smith, the adventurous Levy encouraged

Shepard to theatricalize his most impossible imaginings: "I remember a little conversation we had. When Sam was first starting to write plays, he was writing little, almost chamber plays. When we were working on, I think it was *Red Cross*, Sam was working on something and we were sitting and talking about some scene he wanted to do, and he said, 'I don't think that could be done anyway on the stage. There's no point in doing it.' And I said, 'You should never think that thought when you're a writer'—I don't remember how I put it. I remember saying, 'Look Sam, if you have the idea that you want an elephant to appear on the stage without walking on from the wings, you should just write it and see what happens from it, and then see if there's a way to do it, or a way to make it." And in a way he took it to heart. He wrote *Fourteen Hundred Thousand* after that with snow coming down, this mess on the stage, and the next big thing he wrote, *Sidewinder*, he had this 'elephant' on stage. It was a snake that was supposed to move by itself and there were also two cars, one up on a rack. It somehow got done."

Shepard was involved completely in the off-off scene, "not unlike what he set up for himself later in San Francisco," notes Levy. "He found it a very exciting way to work, and liked being part of it, but he was not a group-oriented person. He hung out with both theater and music people. He didn't feel allegiance like you're a 'Judson playwright' or an 'Open Theater playwright.' He wasn't a joiner, but you didn't have to be."

The Open Theater was working in a unique way and Shepard was undoubtedly impressed with their take on a book which helped form their key concepts in those days—Erving Goffman's *Presentation of Self in Everyday Life*, which was based on a post-Freudian notion that the human personality is built up through a succession of circumstances one finds oneself in. There's an essence to each person, and if one is more or less resilient, one creates oneself additionally for different situations: One is different with the boss than one is with co-workers, and different with co-workers than with a lover. Though it can't be said that Shepard read Goffman's book, the workpool at the Open Theater was a mutual influence, the daily sessions were open, Shepard was a contributing playwright, and one can see that he adopted certain strategies from Goffman's book via the Open Theater. In addition, Shepard obviously owes a debt to the Open Theater's "transformation" exercise, in which actors would quickly change personalities from scene to scene within a single work, often without apparent psychological motivation, moving in and out of characters in much the same way he and Mingus had played with different voices.

Jacques Levy recalls that "Sam would do a lot of watching at the Open Theater. Most of what we did then was exercises. We did some work of other writers: Jean-Claude van Itallie, Megan Terry—there was a bunch that was around. So he did see other people's things. He would come to rehearsals when I was working on his plays—he wouldn't be there every minute —but he came regularly, and we always had a very open relationship with each other, where we would talk about who's not working, what's not working. There wasn't a lot of talking about why, a lot of justifying what we felt. If we didn't like something for some reason, we just didn't like it. Sam was always very open to be shown something he hadn't intended or thought of in his writing. When he wrote *Red Cross* he didn't think of having it all in white, including the groceries and costumes, but when he heard the idea, he said, 'Oh!' "

Shepard's immersion in any experience was only up to a point: He would observe, take what he could use, and make it uniquely his own. Although he enjoyed and profited from his experience with the Open Theater, he resisted some elements of their process. According to Levy, Shepard's work was treated differently than that of other playwrights: "He was writing these short one-act plays—really bursts of writing. I did *Amer-*

ica Hurrah—Joyce was in that—and most of the things were created with the actors. But we didn't do that much with Sam's stuff. He resisted that, although it was there for him to take part in. But he didn't like that. He liked a certain kind of improvisation in the way he wrote—we had a lot of talks about this. One of us said the idea was to stay out of the way of the writing: a metaphor for letting the unconscious or whatever flow. It's never really completely true, of course. And I was into the same thing from the directing viewpoint, as were the actors we were working with, who were becoming very well trained at improvisation—not the Second City type, although sometimes it was funny, wisecracking, but also based on deep insight—and a kind of Brechtian stepping outside to confront the audience or lose the character.

"Sam had some small plays I did in workshop with the actors. They were wonderful and most of them were seen only by a few people. They were fun and one of them was done for public television at one point—*Fourteen Hundred Thousand.*" A play in one act, *Fourteen Hundred Thousand* opens with Tom building a bookcase. The stage is lit in blue light which suddenly changes to white as a shelf falls to the floor. Donna enters with two cans of white paint saying she and Tom cannot go on vacation until the bookcase is complete. Tom complains that her fourteen hundred books are unread, just meant for display. They end up fighting, using the paint brushes as if they were swords. Mom and Pop enter with armloads of books complaining about the climb; they open books and read, oblivious as Donna and Tom charge each other, screaming. Mom and Pop read in unison from their books and Tom and Donna join in with a recitation about a great snowfall which covered everything. The lights change once more and the shelves fall off the bookcase. Mom and Pop stand and read a dissertation on urban living to the background of the other characters humming "White Christmas."

Levy also directed *Red Cross,* another one-act play, concerning Jim and Carol, who are staying in a Red Cross cabin. Carol relates a story of a skiing accident which has completely dismembered her. An offstage voice calls her and she leaves for town. Jim removes his pants and begins picking bugs off his legs and stepping on them. He then does push-ups as the maid comes to change the beds. At first, Jim won't let her in because he's embarrassed by the yellow spots on the sheets, but he relents and, as she works, asks her if she knows anything about crabs. He continues to interrupt her, eventually involving her in a swimming lesson on the beds, during which the maid imagines she is drowning. The maid delivers a monologue about coming out of the water "a new creature" and leaves. Jim puts his pants back on just as Carol returns complaining of bugs all over herself. Jim turns to face her and the audience, revealing a stream of blood running down his forehead.

The lack in Shepard's plays of the kind of ordinary logic we experience in our daily outer lives was difficult for some actors to interpret, as were the long, apparently chaotic monologues. "When we started to work on *Red Cross* together, those long monologues that Sam was always trying to make work—that stream would just carry him off—were always very difficult for the actors," noted Jacques Levy. "Sam wanted them to be treated like musical solos, but that doesn't help an actor—they don't see it from that point of view. But I was able to find a way of getting what the insight of a monologue was so the actor could understand what was going on. Then I would put some overlay on top to give that little bit of distance and it would often make it funnier. In *Red Cross* and *La Turista* there were a bunch of those instances.

"One of the things Joyce, of course, understood was how funny his plays were. She understood where he was coming from. He's a very funny person and so are the people he's been involved with. He could get brutal, crucial, scary—all that in his plays. His funny is different from Pinter or Beckett—not wry—it's a certain abstraction in his humor always, something to do with a certain cool imagination that was in the air in the Sixties. Jack Nicholson should be in a Shepard play."

Levy was also untroubled by Shepard's difficulty in ending his plays, which he considered an honest reflection of the open-ended nature of reality: "It's really terrific. That's part of the price you pay when you try to do some kind of improvisational stuff. You almost never have an ending; it's very hard to find one. Most of his early plays come out of his own experiences, which he expanded and changed, off-slanted, exaggerated, whatever. He would just start going with a group of characters with only a vague idea of where he was going. Sometimes the structure would come out perfectly. He had an intuitive grasp of that, but sometimes it was like a tap dancer not knowing how to finish. And so there are a variety of ways: blood, explosions, fog—I guess the worst is the flying saucer coming down in *Sidewinder*. I loved the fog ending in *Forensic and the Navigators*. In *La Turista* we tried for a long time to get that ending, and finally Sam said, 'He should just disappear.' But it's really that he bolts. So I finally came up with an idea that worked: The actor ran down through the audience, stepped on the stage, went through the back wall, and left this cartoon outline. It was a startling moment and there was nothing left to do in that play.

"You have to understand that people didn't understand what was going on in that play—they were, of course, confused. That's one of the reasons why it took so long for any kind of public acceptance of him. It wasn't until he began to write with a more linear structure that people could understand what was going on.

"At that time he was doing only a little bit of rewriting; he would cut a bit if something was too long or change it if I felt something wasn't working, or if an actor came up with something, he would include that—little stuff, but not major rewriting, until *La Turista.* He originally showed it to me as a three-act play. The first act was pretty much like what we did, but the second act lost the main character and went off and followed the girl, and then the third act went further. We were riding to Philadelphia to see a play, talking, and I said to him that I just couldn't buy that, the first act was a great setup for something, and then it left it hanging. I said he should rewrite it, and he agreed. We'd talk on the phone every once in a while and he'd say he was working on it. Maybe ten days later, he came to me: He'd thrown out the second and third acts and written a new second act which actually took place in time before the first act. I really liked it. It was obviously a very abstract exercise for an audience, and we did some changing in rehearsal, of course, because it was still fresh." One change, according to Wynn Handman, the founder and director of the American Place Theater, where the production took place, was Levy and Shepard's plan to kill a live chicken on stage. New York State forbade that so they had to settle for "sleight of hand."

Handman had begun the American Place Theater in 1964 with the intention of establishing a place where American poets and playwrights could develop their dramatic works with an audience drawn only from subscription, thereby giving the playwright the option of excluding critics from reviewing their work. Their first production, poet Robert Lowell's *The Old Glory,* opened November 1964; their ninth, Sam Shepard's *La Turista,* opened March 4, 1967, starring Joyce Aaron as Salem and Sam Waterston, who has since gone on to a highly successful career on stage and screen, as Kent.

A full-length play in two acts, *La Turista* was inspired by Shepard and Aaron's Mexican trip. Not an easy play to penetrate, *La Turista* concerns shifting identities and mythic roles, using imagery drawn from film and television. Personalities, even race and spatial-temporal realities are in constant flux. Reality and fantasy slide into each other. The second act does not follow the first in time but is an extension and comments upon it. The plot, such as it is, concerns Kent and Salem marooned in a derelict Mexican hotel room suffering from dysentery. A doctor arrives with the cure: the sacrifice of two live chickens. In the second act, the doctor and his son are dressed in Civil War costumes. The play ends as Kent, dressed as a monster, leaps through the back wall of the set.

Once again, it was at Joyce Aaron's suggestion that Handman had come to know Sam Shepard. Handman recalls: "Joyce Aaron, who had been an acting student of mine, told me about this great new playwright, so I went to see *Chicago,* agreed, and when he had written *La Turista,* Joyce told me. We did it in 1967." Shepard elected to exercise his "no critics" option, because he felt being reviewed put too much pressure and too many expectations on the actors during rehearsal period. He wanted the work to be done for its own sake. But Elizabeth Hardwick, wife of member playwright Robert Lowell, was also a subscriber. She loved the play so much that she argued her right to review it under freedom of the press. Ironically, her glowing and insightful review was later cited by Shepard in an application for a grant. She opens: *"La Turista* by Sam Shepard, in a dazzling production at the American Place Theater, is a work of superlative interest." She calls Shepard "one of the three or four gifted playwrights alive," applauding him on his integrity even at her own and other critics' expense: "It is a sacrificial act of the most serious sort. It means nothing less than, after a fixed run, if one is lucky enough to have that, the play may suffer simple cessation for want of those good and bad advertisements combed from the newspapers and television. Perhaps it is only young people, free of deforming ambitions, who would have the courage to submit to such a test. Or perhaps it is the strength of their art that allows them to wait for what will come or not come. There are worse things than silence."[12]

Sam Waterston, who was cast by Jacques Levy in *Red Cross* and *La Turista,* was impressed by Shepard's gifts as well as his integrity: "I had been doing a play on Broadway from which I was fired and was very upset, of course, and within three days of being fired started doing *La Turista.* I had the satisfaction of watching the Broadway play close while I was rehearsing this other one." Like Joyce Aaron, Waterston was unperturbed by Shepard and Levy's unorthodox ways: "It was a combination of working in a Shepard play and working with Jacques, who was very much in the vanguard of what was being done, of how plays were being thought of directorially in those days. I think a lot of that has been absorbed now, but, at that time, there were two traditional ways of approaching a play. One was the 'British way,' and the other was the 'Method way.' And Jacques did whatever way served best—it was a kind of rule-breaking manner of going about things. Both Sam and Jacques didn't explain things like the character does this because of something that happened with his mother when he was a child—he just does it. You don't need to have the history in order to believe in the reality of people's circumstances. For them, the theater itself has a reality of its own and didn't need any kind of linear connection to regular reality in order to be about life— it could connect in a jump. The play just is what it is.

"It was great fun for me as an actor. The invitation from Jacques was: Take a flying leap and it will be okay. I didn't have a whole lot of conversations with Sam about *La Turista,* but he was there pretty much the whole time. He would sit around, go out and come back. He and Jacques talked a lot and Joyce Aaron, his girlfriend, was in it, so it was all very relaxed. He was neither formally excluding himself nor throwing his weight around. It was very much a collaborative thing where Jacques wanted to do what Sam wanted to do and Sam wanted to do what Jacques wanted to do."

Though Shepard had been reluctant to be reviewed, he was open to his audience, and made himself available for after-play discussions which had been instituted by Wynn Handman. "There was a wonderful night when people from Long Island University came in to watch it and have a discussion with the playwright," recalls Waterston. "Sam was up at a podium and they asked, 'What does this mean?' and he would say, 'Well, uh' —very awkward and shy— 'well, what do you think it means?' It was whatever the opposite of an interview is. He was explicitly and implicitly turning it back to them.

"Shepard was very intense, very uncharted, unprogrammed, and, therefore, unpredictable. I didn't see his future written on his face. I would have guessed that he would be his generation's most important playwright, and he was already on his way, but, no, I didn't see him as a movie star. I thought of him as a playwright and a very interesting man."

Although Shepard was uninterested in "legitimate, uptown" success, he was well praised and supported by the downtown community: *Cowboys, Rock Garden, Up to Thursday, Chicago, 4-H Club, Fourteen Hundred Thousand, Icarus's Mother, Dog, Rocking Chair, Red Cross,* and *La Turista* had all been produced by the end of 1967. He had won three Obies for distinguished playwriting—for *Red Cross, Icarus's Mother,* and *Chicago*—and Kevin O'Connor had won an Obie for distinguished acting. Ellen Stewart, the founder of La Mama and the person who most influenced the off-off-Broadway style of theater, used some of her grant money to pay Shepard for serving coffee and hot chocolate to her theater guests. She also gave him a room in which to write and bang on his drums. Stewart sent *Chicago* off to Europe with eight other plays from La Mama, where it enjoyed great success as directed by Tom O'Horgan (who went on to gain fame as the director of *Hair,* the quintessential theatrical expression of the spirit of the Sixties), and starring, once more, Kevin O'Connor as the angry young man in the bathtub.

But Shepard was and remains an experimental and multitalented personality. His success in theater, while satisfying, was not enough. He had been playing his drums with different groups of musicians almost since the moment he arrived in New York, and by 1967 he was recording with the Holy Modal Rounders, whose unique sound blended Steve Weber's pre–World War II blues and Peter Stampfel's pre–World War II country mountain music into something which might be loosely described as psychedelic country rock. As Stampfel describes the Rounders, "It was basically acoustic pre–World War II white and black music put together. We started in 1963, we were the Fugs' first backing band between December 1964 and June 1965, and our first record was made the day before [John] Kennedy was shot.

"I quit playing with Weber in 1965 because he was getting crazed, and I was looking to put together another group and master the art of songwriting with my now ex–old lady, Antonia. In 1966, a friend of ours, Carol—I can't think of her last name, but she was one of the first women on the folk scene who had the chops of a man lead guitar player—said that some guys wanted a Holy Modal Rounders concert for which they'd pay a substantial amount. So, although we had broken up, we got together for this gig. My fiddle was in pawn because I was learning to pay electric bass, so I went into the pawn shop on Second Avenue, and this guy asked, 'Hey, do you know any bass players?' And I said, 'I'm playing electric bass.' I don't know why he asked me because I had this fiddle in my hand that I'd just unpawned. He said he was drumming with this guy who was an electric-guitar player and they had been told they sounded too thin. They needed a bass player and he asked if I was interested. I said, 'Sure.' That guy was Sam and that's how

I met him, in the fall of 1966. I had a group at the time called the Swamp Willies which turned into the Moray Eels, and Sam became the drummer for that, besides my playing with him and the guitar player who was billed as 'the Heavy Metal Kid.'

"In 1967, ESP Records approached us to make a Holy Modal Rounders record and I said, 'Sure,' but I wanted Sam to be drumming on it. At the time Sam was getting very fed up with all the long hair going around and had gotten a crewcut. I wanted us to have our pictures on the album and Bernard Stollman, 'Mr. ESP Records,' didn't want Sam on the album because he didn't look right. He had this short hair and that wasn't done. It was a terrible record because we hadn't played together for a number of years, and the reason I quit playing with Weber was he refused to practice anymore and work out songs. We basically had to throw together an album without playing together for about two years. It was recorded during the Israeli-Egyptian war, oddly enough, and we called it Indian War Whoop after a song recorded in the late Twenties by Floyd Ming and His Pepsteppers. We covered that tune and named the album for it. It was basically me, Weber, and Sam. On the liner notes I wrote: 'Sam Shepard writes plays and drums.' Weber was doing the copy-editing for the liner notes, and he put a comma between *writes* and *plays* because he didn't realize 'writes plays' means 'writes plays.' "

While they achieved a certain cult status, the Holy Modal Rounders did not generate enough income to relieve Shepard from financial concerns. In 1967 he won a Rockefeller Grant, and in 1968 a Guggenheim Fellowship gave him greater freedom to write full-time. But until those grants came through, according to Shepard, there was almost no money: "There wasn't any money at all, until the grants started coming in from Ford and Rockefeller and all these places that were supporting the theatres because of the publicity they started getting. Then they began paying the actors and playwrights—but it wasn't much, one hundred dollars for five weeks' work or something.

"I never thought of it as my job, because it was something that made me feel more relaxed, whereas I always thought of jobs as something that made you feel less alive—you know, the thing of working ten hours a day cleaning horseshit out of a stable."[13]

Shepard considered himself professional enough, however, to engage the services of a literary agent, Toby Cole, who had edited *Playwrights on Playwrighting, Acting: A Handbook of the Stanislavski Method, Actors on Acting,* and *Directing the Play.* By Shepard's own admission, Cole functioned as much more than a literary agent in his career. She understood his genius, respected his desire to maintain the integrity of his work by avoiding commercialism despite his continual need of funds, and functioned as an all-around motherly muse. Producer-manager Albert Poland calls her "one of the great agents because she had genuine substance. She was a kind of Thirties radical who represented almost anybody you could think of who had any substance of any kind politically or socially or as an artist. Sam adored her."

One of the first things she did was to make use of her contacts to get Shepard's grant applications pushed through, citing his contract with Bobbs-Merrill to publish *Five Plays,* the production of his first full-length play, *La Turista,* and the rave review (which almost didn't happen) of that play by Elizabeth Hardwick in the *New York Review of Books.*

By spring 1967 Shepard was no longer living with Joyce Aaron. He and his new girl, an astrologer named Nancy, shared an apartment on Sixth Avenue and Prince Street with its tenant, Bill Hart, whom Shepard had met through Aaron: "We met in Pennsylvania," Hart recalls. "Michael Smith was running something down there, and by accident he just came in with Joyce Aaron, whom I knew at the time. I think they had been in Mexico. We spent a lot of the afternoon telling stories to each other. I was doing some acting and writing but was just there with friends. We never said a word about theater: just exchanged personal tales—played tennis without a ball—fooled around and laughed a lot. Then I saw him a couple of times on the street, and one day Joe Chaikin [founder of the Open Theater] called me and said Sam was looking for a place to stay. He was staying with Joe but he didn't have enough room. I had a lot of space, so Sam came over and said, 'Maybe we could work something out—I could pay half the rent.' It wasn't like taking a guy off the street. He already had his grants. I said, 'Okay,' and he stayed until he met O-Lan, when they moved to an apartment downstairs."

Hart is one of the few early friends who have remained close with Shepard to this day, which Hart attributes to the fact that their relationship is not one of work: "It's personal. We were friends and we've been friends ever since the first day we met, and it hasn't been fucked up by a lot of bullshit. I leave him alone and he leaves me alone. I did direct the New York premieres of two of his plays, *Shaved Splits* and *Cowboys #2,* which he gave to me."

Cowboys #2, a revised version of *Cowboys,* opens with two young men, not unlike Shepard and his "pardner" Charles Mingus, leaning against a wall discussing the possibility of rain. They take turns playing an old-timer surveying the clouds and watching a rainstorm, then building their fantasy into a prairie night and an Indian attack. Stu, who plays Clem in this fantasy, gets shot by an arrow, and Chet, who is playing Mel, fires on the imaginary Indians and throws real water on Stu's imaginary wounds. Stu, angered, stops the game, then soaks his feet in the stream Chet created at the side of the stage as he talks about how things have changed. We hear car horns in the background as Chet begins a long monologue on breakfast foods. Two men converse from the wings across the stage as the car horns increase in volume. Chet tries unsuccessfully to wake Stu and begins to assume his old-man character more and more as he tries to keep the vultures from the body of his friend. The car horns are joined by the sounds of an Indian attack, and just before Chet's long final monologue ends, the two men from the wings enter and begin reciting the play from the beginning.

Shaved Splits, a parody of both revolutionaries and the effete wealthy elite, also plays with the notion that both our lives and art are equally real and unreal. A wealthy woman who lives on chocolate and pornography is held prisoner by a young revolutionary. She is wounded, she watches her husband get shot down by the authorities, and her servant performs Balinese dances before jumping out the window.

Shepard and Hart did work together one time, on a movie Hart made. "It has some extraordinary scenes, mostly about black power," says Hart. "Joyce Aaron, Charles Mingus, and a lot of black people are in it. We wrote some, and much of it was improvised. We shot it mainly in my apartment, some in Harlem, and some in taxicabs going back and forth on mysterious routes. A lot of it is about white people aping black styles and how blacks are resentful of a lot of things. I was trying to get a lot of that stuff out there. It's very upsetting material and it was very on time, but we ran out of money and I ran out of discipline."

According to Mingus, "The movie had several incredible scenes—its concept was you can do it in one take if the take is perceived as a form and the take would be an entire reel, about ten minutes. The whole movie was a series of improvisations that Bill connected together but then failed to complete, but individual segments were movies in themselves. Like, Sam and I and Joyce did one where we worked out any hostilities, any confusion, any emotional confrontations."

Shepard later transformed the experience of the film in the same piece in which he reworked Aaron's acid trip: " 'What you been doin' Billy,' " the narrator asks his friend, who lives "right next to the Police Warehouse on Sixth Avenue," as Shepard and Hart in fact did. " 'Me? I abandoned my film.' 'The one with Charlie?' 'Yeah, that one.' 'The one where Charlie rips the head off the dove?' 'Yeah, that one.' 'What happened?' 'I lost the continuity.' "[14]

Mingus recalls that his and Shepard's lives "more or less drifted apart during the filming of Hart's movie. I became a painter and he became a playwright. I was involved in a world of painters, musicians, parties, and cocktail circuits—a little more bullshit. He was really a serious, nine-to-five type of writer."

Shepard may have been a "nine-to-five" writer, but after hours he not only continued jamming with other musicians, he also tentatively picked up his neglected acting career. After visiting "The Farm," an old abandoned dairy farm near Strasburg, Pennsylvania, where Theater Genesis people would hang out and make theater, Shepard did a little more acting, albeit in an unorthodox style. Genesis playwrights Murray Mednick and Tony Barsha were developing a piece: "Something we called *The Vision Piece* or *The Body Piece*—we never did have a name for it," says Barsha. "It was one of those hippie-type communal pieces. It was fun: Murray and I were structuring and directing it, and bringing information in, and the actors were putting in the dialogue. We were all just hanging out at this farm we had had for a few years—a whole bunch of us went out there. Scarlett Johnson and her daughter, O-Lan, were in it. I was going with O-Lan at the time Sam met her, and he was with Nancy, an astrologer. Sam had been visiting the farm. He said he wanted to do some acting—he didn't want to do any writing, and he was very good. It was one of those experimental pieces without much dialogue, a lot of carrying on with magical stuff—Kabbalah and Indian stuff—like some Living Theater pieces, but smaller, more intimate, so it was more like a more intimate *Paradise Now.* It was a big hit, a big success. Just a star was painted on the floor and the audience would get involved. There were things like somebody had an epileptic fit and one of the actors got in and did the fit with him and brought him out of it. Some guy had seen a war protester set himself on fire in Central Park and he came in and related that. I don't remember anything in particular Sam did, just he was very energetic, he had a lot of energy. O-Lan seemed to have a problem projecting, making things large, but she was good. Sam was so crazy, he didn't have any problems. He wasn't such a good actor, but he had such an energetic personality.

"It was during that time that O-Lan and Sam got together —she was my girlfriend."

FOUR

Born to an actress mother who seems to have named her after a character in Pearl Buck's *The Good Earth,* O-Lan impresses everyone who knows her with her sweet earthiness: "Like a little Hell's Angelette," writer Robert Coe thought. Missing teeth, vivacious with a gleeful, maniacal edge, O-Lan is adorable and completely unglamorous in her Levi's and leather jacket. In image, at least, she was Shepard's female counterpart. Jacques Levy recalls her as "very sweet, very funny, with a terrific sense of the ridiculous. She could make comments which in someone else's mouth would be wisecracks, but in hers would come out as sweet innocence. Although she is very bright, she could play it dumb. One sequence in Shepard's *Forensic and the Navigators* is created out of her life: She puts her hand on the Rice Krispies so they won't go out of the bowl and then pours the milk over her hand. It was a wonderful moment. O-Lan would know that was funny and she would go that extra-ridiculous step because she knew it was funny."

Like Joyce Aaron, O-Lan is a unique, gifted, strong character, and, according to Levy, her "influence was also considerable because so many of [Sam's] female characters were based on or connected to her. She informed them one way or another, and when she played them, they would become set."

Forensic and the Navigators was first produced at Theater Genesis in December 1967. Ralph Cook directed Lee Kissman,

Walter Hadler, and Beeson Carrol, three actors who regularly worked in Shepard's plays, as well as O-Lan, playing the character she obviously inspired, Oolan. Another satire of both revolutionaries and the establishment, *Forensic and the Navigators* portrays a somewhat confused struggle between two revolutionaries and the Exterminators, who are agents for an unnamed power holding people in a nearby prison camp. Neither side is very resolute in this struggle, as they are easily distracted by the charms of a young girl, Oolan. As they drift in their confusion, they are destroyed by a cloud of colored gas which covers the stage and billows out over the audience. The foes remain in an interminable state of stasis.

In the same year *Forensic* was produced, Bobbs-Merrill published a collection of Shepard's plays, containing an unproduced play, *Melodrama Play,* which, together with *Forensic,* won an Obie for the 1968 season.

A grim play in which Duke Durgens, a songwriter with one big hit tune to his credit, is being brutalized by his manager and brother in an effort to "inspire" another hit, *Melodrama Play* reflects Shepard's burgeoning disenchantment with New York and what he felt was its insular theater scene, a feeling which was exacerbated by the difficulties he had getting an uncompromised off-Broadway production of *La Turista.* Making theater was beginning to resemble shoveling horseshit—it was beginning to be a job. "When I first got to New York," says Shepard, "it was wide open, you were like a kid in a fun park, but then as it developed, as more and more elements came into it, things got more and more insane—you know, the difference between living in New York and working in New York got wider and wider, so that you were doing this thing called *theatre* in these little places and you were bringing your so-called experience to it, and then going back and living in this kind of tight, insular, protective way, where you were defending yourself."[1]

In an essay anthologized in *American Dreams,* Shepard

wrote, "The reason I began writing plays was the hope of extending the sensation of *play* (as in 'kid') on into adult life. If 'play' becomes 'labor,' why play?"[2]

Shortly after it won the Obie, Tom O'Horgan directed *Melodrama Play* with his own musical score at La Mama; it was the first of Shepard's original productions where he was not present at rehearsals, slouching in a back row seat, squinting up at the stage and giggling at his own lines.

Melodrama Play is also the first of Shepard's works to reflect in its content his strong involvement with the music scene, with which the musically talented O-Lan was even more familiar. He played drums for *Melodrama Play* when it opened even though he had kept away from rehearsals, and he had kept playing with Peter Stampfel of the Holy Modal Rounders and the Moray Eels, as well as others. Shepard had a particular admiration for Mick Jagger of the Rolling Stones, with whom he was soon to fulfill—or almost—a rock 'n' roll playwright's fantasy.

Nineteen sixty-eight was a wildly exciting year for Shepard, fertile and full of opportunities and challenges. Unfortunately, it also contained the seeds of great frustration. Michelangelo Antonioni, the great Italian filmmaker, asked Shepard to script his first film set and shot in America, *Zabriskie Point.* Since its subject was young American revolutionaries and it involved an airplane, it was apparently fitting that Antonioni would call upon America's premier Angry Young Man playwright, who, as it happened, had even written a play involving an airplane *(Icarus's Mother).* "He got in touch with me," Shepard told the *Village Voice.* "He came to New York looking for writers for this scenario and he read my plays. I had a play called *Icarus's Mother,* which had an airplane in it; he figured that since he had an airplane in his movie we had something in common." Shepard went to Rome to work on the script with Antonioni, and, for the first time, luxuriated in comparatively big money and a liberal expense account, courtesy of the producing studio,

MGM. Both Shepard and Antonioni were blissfully ignorant of the fact that ideologically they were poles apart: Antonioni, following the fashion of the chic European left, was rhapsodic about the emerging American radical left, while Shepard held both the establishment and the rabble-rousing revolutionaries equally in contempt.

At the same time that Shepard and Antonioni and assorted others were busily working out a script, Cole was negotiating with Ted Mann for a Broadway production, possibly at the Henry Miller Theater, of one of Shepard's plays. Though he was excited at the prospect, Shepard never wavered from his primary concern that his work be served: He was adamantly opposed to a double bill with ordinary Broadway pap, insistent that Jacques Levy, whom he trusted, direct, and that no changes be made other than those authorized by either Levy or himself. The negotiations did not work out, further nurturing Shepard's growing disenchantment with "professional" theater.

Offers were pouring in—including a request to script *Alice's Restaurant,* the quintessential Sixties hippie movie starring Arlo Guthrie—but Shepard's commitment to Antonioni overrode them all.

While Shepard was in Rome, however, he met a man who asked him to help script a movie for the Rolling Stones. Thrilled, Shepard went off to Keith Richards's English estate to work on the film, to be called *Maxagasm.*

Opportunity seemed to be not merely politely knocking at his door but banging and screaming to be let in. Shepard welcomed the risk and adventure, but when he opened the door, he stepped through into thin air—a sheer drop. Everything fell through. Shepard never made it to Broadway—in fact, he never has, and deliberately so. The Rolling Stones film was never produced, and the Antonioni period was, at best, a lesson hard learned. "Antonioni contacted Shepard because he wanted a writer who understood American idiom, but he didn't understand that what Shepard wrote was Shepard's," says Bill Hart. "I think almost all of it was not used, but Shepard never made a big deal about it, he never fussed." The writing credits ended up listing Shepard, Antonioni, Fred Gardner, Clare Peploe, and Tonino Guerra. Shepard made an unsuccessful attempt to protest the credits, but it was no great loss: As one reviewer put it, the film was bad enough "to give anti-Americanism a bad name."

In the *Village Voice* interview Shepard himself spoke of the Antonioni experience as a disaster: "I wrote the very first version of *Zabriskie Point,* and as Antonioni got into it, he got more and more politically oriented. I didn't want anything to do with it, so I dropped out of that. However, he used quite a bit of my original stuff, up to the point where it begins to speak for radical politics.

"Antonioni wanted to make a political statement about contemporary youth, write in a lot of Marxist jargon and Black Panther speeches. I couldn't do it. I just wasn't interested.

"Plus I was twenty-four and just wasted by the experience. It was like a nightmare, I was surrounded by MGM and all that stuff.

"I like Michelangelo a lot—he is incredible—but to submerge yourself in that world of limousines and hotels and rehashing and pleasing Carlo Ponti is just . . . forget it. I spent two years, off and on, around the whole business."

Though Shepard's work on *Zabriskie Point* was over when they began the shoot in Los Angeles, he spent time on the set. Michael Smith, the *Village Voice* critic whose rave review had sparked Shepard's early success, remembers visiting Shepard on the set: "It was funny—they had a whole sleek office set built up on a roof of a building in downtown Los Angeles, and they were waiting for the weather to be clear enough so they could get a shot of some building in the background. A typical movie day where they stand around and wait.

"Sam was playing with the Holy Modal Rounders at the time and sharing a house with them somewhere in Los Angeles. He was more involved with that and was just hanging around the movie set that day, checking in out of curiosity rather than working on it."

The Holy Modal Rounders had been asked by a record producer who went by the name of Frazier Mohawk to make a record for Elektra Records in 1968, which they wanted to record in Los Angeles. "Sam was supposed to work on Antonioni's *Zabriskie Point* in Los Angeles," recalls Peter Stampfel, "so obviously it was the right time to go there. So we made a record which was another sloppy mess. Again, Weber didn't want to rehearse for it. I explained to the producer that the reason the previous record sounded so wacked out was that we hadn't practiced before getting to the studio and somebody basically had to hold a whip hand on Weber, make him actually work on the songs before going into the studio. When we got there, Frazier Mohawk said, 'I'm going to talk to Weber. He'll be fine.' And, of course, Weber wasn't fine, and the record was another mess. Those two records, unfortunately, are the only two Sam was on and they were greatly flawed by the way things happened at the time, Weber having been in this recalcitrant period. Also, both the producers of the ESP and Elektra records had this identical wacky, acid-flash, psychedelic idea: They wanted to make a record without the grooves. What happens when the radio station wants to play the third song? How do they find it? How can you get radio play? How can you sell records?

"But Sam did a very interesting Pledge of Allegiance on the Elektra record. (Both records are very interesting in an anarchistic way, in terms of how much can be gotten away with.) The only thing they really liked was Sam's piece. I wanted to record 'America the Beautiful' because everyone was hating America at the time, and I thought it would be a very hip move to do a real serious version of 'America the Beautiful.' And it turned into a mess because no one knew the words except me and I wanted a chorus singing it, and you can't have a chorus if no one knows the words. So we played it and Sam recited the Pledge of Allegiance over it, which he couldn't remember the words to either. So, in the middle, he goes into this whole thing, 'I forgot the words, I forgot the words! I'm going to get an F! Mom! Pop!' It was really nice, it's the last piece on that album.

"So then Elektra wanted to make a record if Sam was in charge of it and if it was a series of sort of comedy bits that Sam wrote. I wanted to make a record of old songs with grooves between the songs, but they weren't interested. And also the band was such an addled, drug-crazed mess at the time, Sam excluded.

"I've read things about how he was a wild drug-taker during the Sixties, but he never was. I never saw him even smoke marijuana—he didn't like it. He always disliked the whole hippie-type image. When we played a couple of colleges, a lot of the girls thought he was a greaser because he had short hair and he wore a leather jacket. He obviously was not a hip person. He was looked on like a low-class hitter type—that's the way a lot of girls pegged him in 1969."

While Shepard and the Rounders were staying in Los Angeles, the Rolling Stones were staying at the Chateau Marmont, "the cool place on the Strip," Stampfel recalls. "Sam came over the house where we used to practice one day with an advance copy of 'Jumping Jack Flash'—it was really exciting. He was also talking about the movie he was doing with the Stones, *Maxagasm*. When we got back to New York in 1969, this got to be a more fun thing for him than playing with the Rounders, so he decided to go to England to work on the movie. We went on to do the music for the Vivian Beaumont production of *Operation Sidewinder* at Lincoln Center in early 1970, but he didn't play. Not much happened after that. Sam did some musical things with a couple of people in the Rounders, like Robin Remialy did the music for *Mad Dog Blues* and Paul Connolly of Lothar and the Hand People did the music for *The Unseen Hand.* Sam had gone to other things, so we got another drummer who was a friend of the bass player. We couldn't tell him to take a walk because Sam was coming back, and, besides, Sam was involved with other things.

"Basically he was perfect to work with—no ego problems, always impatient whenever things weren't moving. We used to refer to him as the ultimate foe of terminal stasis because he was basically a person that we used to call in the Sixties a 'motion person,' always making things happen, and things *would* happen around him.

"During a period we were feuding with a guitar player in the Moray Eels who broke up the band to do a gig in which he was the lead singer, the band broke up and got together again. And when Sam came back to play with us, there was this loud pounding on the door. We opened it and Sam walked in carrying his entire drum kit. I don't know how he managed to carry the whole thing, but he did it. He walked in saying in this high voice, 'Home again, home again, jiggety jig, home again, home again, jiggety jig.' "

According to Stampfel, Shepard was a good player: "He would tend not to do the same thing twice much, but the whole band wasn't into keeping steady parts. He always pushed the beat—defined and pushed it.

"He wrote this one incredible song called 'Blind Rage,' which is really a total punk song, in 1969. The last time I saw him, I asked him if he had the words. He performed it a couple of times with the band—playing the drums and singing. He had started playing guitar and writing songs in about 1969. Someone showed him how to do chords on piano and he started playing piano, as well, just like that. When he started out playing guitar, he began writing some really nice songs, but from what I gather, in the Seventies he got more interested in jazz than in rock 'n' roll."

With his theatrical star ever on the rise and the promise of making a movie with his musical heroes, the Rolling Stones, even the "ultimate foe of terminal stasis" had to choose his commitments, and Shepard appeared to make all the right choices.

Maxagasm, the film Shepard wrote for the Rolling Stones, had seemed full of promise and close to realization, but the death of Brian Jones, who had been heavily involved in the project, dampened everyone's enthusiasm, and the project died with him.

Shepard's work on another film, *Me and My Brother,* which he wrote with filmmaker Robert Frank, was more satisfactory. It was becoming more and more evident to Shepard that working on a smaller scale with friends who shared his vision gave him the artistic freedom that comes with control. Bill Hart, the theater director who had shared his apartment with Shepard before his marriage to O-Lan, calls the film "extraordinary. It should be seen by more people. There was some contribution of writing there, but that was like when you would work with the Open Theater—you would contribute some material. But he's written a number of screenplays which the studios just don't know what to do with."

Shepard told the *Voice,* "I've enjoyed working with Robert. And I've written a lot of stuff for other people, but that never got done. I wrote a script for Tony Richardson called *Bodyguard.*" Later, Shepard worked anonymously as a staff writer in Hollywood—an experience which led to the humorous, fantastical indictment of Los Angeles movie-making, *Angel City.*

Shepard was always extremely interested in writing for the movies, and, obviously, that interest has not waned. He took courses in filmmaking with Mike Rohmer, Robert Young, and Stanley Kauffmann at Yale University under a fellowship set up by ABC Television, which hoped to groom the original talents of off-off Broadway for a convention-bound medium which could never accommodate them. Shepard took the train to New Haven twice a week with fellow playwrights Rochelle Owens, Megan Terry, and Kenneth H. Brown—an extraordinary group all eager to learn about screenwriting.

The influence of Shepard's experiences with film was evident in the form and content of his first three-act play, *Operation Sidewinder,* which grew out of a trip he had taken to the desert before he had gone off to Rome to work with Antonioni.

According to Peter Stampfel, while the Holy Modal Rounders were rehearsing for the Elektra album, Shepard was writing *Operation Sidewinder:* "A lot of the songs we were practicing at the time seemed to segue neatly into the plot of *Sidewinder,* so he wrote the songs into the play." Composed of twelve satirical scenes divided by rock music interludes played by the Rounders, *Sidewinder* contrasts the shallowness of mainstream America with the deep culture of one of its original native peoples, the Hopi Indians. The plot concerns a state-of-the-art Air Force computer shaped like a sidewinder snake which has escaped into the desert and is fought over by the power-mad military and black revolutionaries who plan to use drugs to undermine and capture the country. An Indian tribe captures the computer, however, giving it the power of spiritual rule with the assistance of extraterrestrials. The moment of apocalypse is imminent, and only those who have a glimmer of spiritual consciousness are rescued by the beings from outer space.

Michael Feingold, the *Village Voice* theater critic, was literary manager at Yale University's drama department at the time the play was submitted there for production. "It was a very touchy political time," he says. "We were going to do *Sidewinder* at Yale, but a lot of objections were raised by the black students in the drama school about the way the black revolutionary characters were treated. In that draft of the script, they were sort of white paranoid-fantasy creatures. There were grounds for objections, but they weren't made in a gracious way. It was a period when black people weren't disposed to being gracious and they had their reasons. There was a big ruckus about the play and Robert Brustein, head of the drama school, tried to stand his ground and hold out for freedom of speech. What happened ultimately was Shepard was sick to death of the controversy, withdrew his rights, and the play surfaced the next season at Lincoln Center. In between there were considerable revisions."

Jacques Levy had been asked to direct the production, but didn't like the play: "I felt badly because I never like to say that to somebody that I've worked with and want to work with. But he took it all right." Michael Schultz, who went on to make the films *Cooley High* and *Car Wash*, took over. According to Feingold, the ending is different: "By the time it was done in Lincoln Center, the whole revolutionary thing was outworn, so [Schultz] made it a comic motif by having it in a drive-in. The revolutionaries come up and a white carhop wonderfully played by Kathy Burns spouts a whole black revolutionary rap to them. I don't know if it was one of Michael's ideas—he's a very smart man—it was wittily done."

Black radicals were not the only group who raised objections to *Sidewinder*. Don Plumley, the actor who had directed Shepard in *The Eggs of the Devil* when he first came to New York, was cast as the lead, Mickey Free, a character based on a real renegade, a half Indian–half white who tracked down outlaws for the government, retired to isolation in Mexico, and refused to speak anything other than English. "But the character in *Sidewinder* has nothing to do with that," explains Plumley. "It's based on Hopi legends. In fact the Hopis came and requested we stop using real corn for the Kachina, which is a god represented by a mask. We had to cut the mask also because the Kachina is an unseen force in Hopi legend, so they wouldn't let us create something which they had never seen or realized. They do have their masks, but they consider that for themselves."

The production was probably Shepard's greatest disappointment to date, generally recognized as a failure even by his staunchest defenders. Designed in such a way as to give the Holy Modal Rounders a Broadway launching, the play and their suite of songs had grown together, along with Shepard's application of cinematic technique to the theater—a somewhat misguided experiment, as Shepard later admitted in an interview with the *Village Voice:* "That single-frame-editing kind of thing doesn't work on stage," he said. "It was very static."

It seemed that this dynamic period in which he attempted new means of self-expression yielded little more than frayed nerves and disappointments. Shepard's most successful efforts remained on a small, noncommercial scale: O'Horgan's tours with groups of plays including *Chicago, Melodrama Play,* and a new one, *The Holy Ghostly,* were great successes throughout Europe, Canada, and America. *Up to Thursday, Red Cross,* and *Chicago* had all received off-Broadway productions, but, as Shepard complained to Kevin O'Connor, "Christ, I've had all these shows done off-off-Broadway and these shows done off-Broadway, and the ones done off-off were better."

In 1969, Shepard's personal life underwent a radical change —O-Lan became pregnant. On November 9, she and Shepard were married by Reverend Michael Allen at St. Mark's Church, home of Theater Genesis. Bill Hart was best man. Patti Gaul, an actress who was working with O-Lan at the time, describes the event as "a very sweet wedding, very Sixties. I believe they had guitar players. It was low-key people in jeans. I remember I was shocked at O-Lan's mother, Scarlett—she seemed so young. She was in jeans and had a suede vest with fringe, and I thought to myself, 'Boy! My mother is not like that!' She was really kind of cool. O-Lan was wearing a long Empire-waist yellow dress with flowers in a kind of wreath in her hair. She was a doll and very bright. They seemed to me to be a perfect pair: They suited each other and looked like they loved each other so much. They seemed like innocent children together, but also both obviously very talented and hip too. It was very sweet and very low-key. The church was full, but it's small. Except for a couple of family members, it was mainly the theatrical community. There was a little reception outside." Their son, Jesse Mojo, was born in 1970.

With a wife and child, Shepard was increasingly conscious that New York City was not the place for a country man and his family. As soon as he was able, he purchased a secluded piece of property—a farm in Nova Scotia—but soon that part-time retreat would not be enough.

Around the time he married, Shepard had begun working in the basement of La Mama with some actors, improvising on a new play, *The Unseen Hand,* while O-Lan was rehearsing another play for La Mama, *Sprintorgasmics,* by German playwright Wilhelm Pevny. *The Unseen Hand* concerned a character named Blue Morphan who is living in a derelict 1951 Chevy by a highway just outside Azusa ("everything from A to Z in the U.S.A."), California. He considers himself more of a creature of the Old West than of the present and is visited by a galaxy traveler named Willie the Space Freak.

The sci-fi Western came to the attention of young producer Albert Poland, who brought in Yale director Jeff Bleckner, made a few cast changes, and moved the show off-Broadway to the Astor Place Theater, where it opened on April 1, 1970, on a double bill with *Forensic and the Navigators,* a month after the Lincoln Center debacle.

Shepard had met Poland through his friend Toby Cole, Shepard's agent. "It seemed to be a lot of things at once," recalls Poland. "I kept hearing about Sam from the people who were in my shows and the people who wrote the things I was producing. And then there was a Sunday article in the *Times* about Sam and Ed Bullins. It was during that time when *Times* headlines always ended with a question mark—they didn't want to commit to anything. The headline on this one was 'America's Great Hopes—White and Black?' So I read about him in that, and thought, 'Well, I should look into this.' I went to Philadelphia and saw a production of *La Turista* which Lee Kissman was in, who was in a lot of things of Sam's and was a good friend of his. I thought it was great, but it had already been done in New York, so I asked Toby to give me any scripts that [Sam] would consider having produced off-Broadway. She gave me a new script he called *Back Bog Beast Bait,* and another called *The Holy Ghostly,* and another called *Forensic and the Navigators.* It was like a speed trip, very funny and paranoid, and ended with the whole theater filling with steam—you couldn't see your hand in front of your face, which appealed to me at that time. I didn't like *Back Bog* very much, but I thought everything would be fine. I spoke to Toby about directors and she said there was a young director at Yale who was going to direct *Sidewinder,* which was canceled because the Black Panthers put pressure on them. His name was Jeff Bleckner and she said, 'Why don't you look into him?' It was his New York debut and he's gone on to win two Emmy awards, one for 'Hill Street Blues' and the other for the special about Alger Hiss. He was a super director and so we decided he would direct *Forensic* and *Back Bog.*

"We were having auditions and Sam came. I noticed that as we were reading *Back Bog,* he was walking up and down the aisle, not looking pleased. He turned to me and said, 'I don't know about this play.' Then somebody finished and he turned to me and said, 'This sounds like bad Tennessee Williams.' At the end of that, he said, 'Albert, I'm pulling this because I don't like the play now that I hear it.' He had another play he was directing himself called *The Unseen Hand:* They were rehearsing in this little room in the basement of La Mama, so he had Jeff and me come to a run-through of it. The room was so tiny it happened on top of us. It was like an acid trip. I think it fit in nicely with Sam's plans because he had taken it as far as I think he wanted to. Part of what he liked about directing was playing poker with the people who weren't on stage while the other actors were going through their thing. He loved to hang out and play poker, and I think he'd begun to lose interest in directing. Sam said, 'Since Jeff is committed to directing the off-Broadway production that we're doing, why doesn't he take over here at La Mama'—because it hadn't gone on yet there— 'and we can use the La Mama to raise money for the off-Broadway production.' So that's what we did.

"The production was not a success—it ran a month. I don't think it was because we changed some of the actors. The reviewers seemed to find fault with the play because we had a group of old critics. And Clive Barnes, who's later gone on to become a champion of Sam's, said that Sam wrote good, disposable plays and compared them to Kleenex. Barnes did a summary of it in one of those yearbooks about off-Broadway that year and said among the plays that deserved longer runs was Sam Shepard's *The Unseen Hand.* And then, when it was revived, he gave it a very fine review, saying 'I'm told I didn't like this play the first time around.' But I announced in *Variety* I was going to write a play about Clive Barnes. I *actually* said I'm writing a play called *The Further Adventures of C.B.,* but I denied that it was about Clive Barnes; I said it is about an elephant that will be played by a gas-filled balloon."

Some of those involved with the La Mama and Astor Place productions preferred the off-off-Broadway version, possibly because the original actors had developed the play together: They were close friends, and their camaraderie strengthened the play's relationships (three of the four characters were brothers). The actors who were left behind when the play moved to the Astor Place felt cheated of the rewards of a work they'd had a hand in developing.

"I remember when I saw the show in performance at La Mama," recalls Poland, "one of the actors literally came at me. He looked like he was near psychosis and he said, 'We've got an attorney, man, in case you don't want to take the whole cast.' There were a lot of drugs. I went to a party at Beeson Carrol's house and Sticks Carlton had his head in the icebox. Another time Richard Lamparski was dying to meet Sam. When I met Richard he was a pornographer, a man of great style, selling pornography to the elite, the crème de la crème of the business world. He got busted about the same time as Lenny Bruce and that woman who ran the House of Fantasy in New Jersey, where they found the head of AT&T dressed as Little Bo Peep. The three of them went on trial and Richard got three months on Riker's Island. Prison affected him very deeply, because he came out and took the straight and narrow. He did all these books called *Whatever Became of . . .* He's a millionaire now, he has a syndicated radio show of the same thing.

"Well, he wanted to meet Sam, and he had a sort of Noel Coward air about him in spite of having sold pornography. So I arranged to bring Sam and the whole La Mama cast over to Richard's house after one of the performances. They headed for the refrigerator—somebody got a gallon of ice cream and polished that off; somebody pulled down the drapes; another person spent the evening on the telephone; another person did number two in the bathroom, which in Richard's house was taboo."

The trials of Albert Poland were not over. "Sam knew this guy Joey Skaggs," Poland continues. "Joey was definitely a Sixties 'dude.' We all hung out at St. Adrian's Bar, and Sam thought Joey could do the poster for our show, but he didn't. However, Joey had these paintings, so we decided to put his paintings in the lobby. The lobby of the Astor Place is big, and we decided we wanted to do a number in it. I said to Sam, 'What's your fantasy on this?' I think we'd already decided on a rock band: we got Lothar and the Hand People, which had been an existing group, but Sam played drums on this occasion. He was wonderful. We had a popcorn machine and we sold Abba Zabba bars and Moxie, which is a soft drink you can only get in Massachusetts—because that's what he wanted to do.

"I knew we were in trouble when the critics arrived: The band was playing and Richard Watts of the *Post* came up to me and I said, 'It's really nice to see you, Dick.' He said, 'Yes, it's nice to see you—I wish I could hear you.'

"So Joey's paintings were there in the lobby. Joey had done things like send a busload of hippies to Queens and build a glacier out of plexiglass and put it in the Hudson—that type of thing. He was a real Dadaist. Joey said he wanted to talk to me. We had drinks at St. Adrian's and he said he wanted someone to kidnap Leo Castelli, the art dealer, and force him to come to the theater and look at his paintings. I sat there trying to maintain an exterior of calm. You have to realize this was still the Sixties—1970, but still the Sixties. Being a manager was a real adventure in those times; people didn't come in frightened of you or in favor of you or anything.

"Opening night, April first, 1970, Sam, Jeff, and I were standing in the back of the theater, watching the critics and the audience vanish as this wall of smoke, which was burning baby oil, came to the back of the theater for the ending of *Forensic*. We were jumping up and down on that one. About a minute later, I turned around and a Rolls Royce pulled up in front of the theater and out of it got about six guys in double-breasted pinstripe suits carrying violin cases. And one of them was Joey Scaggs. I thought, 'Hmmmmmm . . . ,'" but none of them was Leo Castelli. So I came in and just as the smoke was clearing and the audience and critics were filing out, the six guys grabbed Sam. It was their intent to kidnap him, put him on a bus, and force him to go to Azusa, California, where the play took place. Well, Sam, you know . . . there was a fist fight between Sam and these six people. The fight broke up and the guys, looking very downhearted, left."

According to Tony Barsha, who was one of the six "gangsters" (and O-Lan's former boyfriend), they were staging an event: "This was Joey's idea—Joey is always getting people in trouble. Sam went crazy, nuts, started throwing punches all over the place, and O-Lan was freaking out in the basement. They recognized me and maybe they thought I was out to revenge myself."

As if this opening weren't electric enough, the party at Silver's on Union Square topped the evening in the only way possible. According to Poland, "It was the 'in' place at the time. They said, 'Do you want a band?' and we said no, but we got a band anyway. The guy who ran it was like a gangster—I mean, he was really fierce. We were supposed to have this opening party until around two, and he called me up in his office upstairs. He looked crazed: 'You guys gotta get out of here.' I said, 'Why? We're supposed to be here all night.' He said, 'Out! Out! I mean business—out!' So we got out and at four in the morning, the building blew up. The Black Panther headquarters were in that building. That was our opening night, and that was Sam's first full production off-Broadway.

"He was rewriting constantly during rehearsals and previews, and he was very much involved," Poland continues. "I remember one time somebody got his foot caught in the curtain, the backdrop, and pulled it aside: There was Sam behind it working the smoke machine. He sang in the band, too. I would describe his singing as Mick Jagger combined with country. It's very simple. Mick Jagger was an idol of his and a friend, too. There was a play by Heathcliff Williams called *AC/DC* done in Brooklyn and I sent Sam to see it because I thought he'd love it. Michael David called me the next afternoon and said, 'Why did you send Sam Shepard here?' I said, 'I thought he'd love it.' He said, 'Well, he stomped out during the first act, screaming "You can't say that about Mick!"' because they had some things in it that were a little bit against Mick Jagger.

"Sam's got more than duality—he's got duality times three. And he's got very childlike elements to him. Yet, of course, he was smart as a whip, too. His response to that Jagger thing, that was like a kid whose hero got attacked.

"After the play ran, I'd run into Sam, talk to him on the phone occasionally. I did a book called the *Off-Off Broadway Book,* in which I did everybody's thumbnail biography in the back through interviewing, so I interviewed him for that. Sam carried with him his mystique—he always had a mystique. He was always very, very aloof from the press and very, very infatuated with heroes, American folk heroes, even Mae West and Paul Bunyan. He liked personas, and had a persona of his own, so it's not surprising to me that he became a movie star. I think that was just the natural unfolding of his life. I don't think he's ever been a careerist; he's followed the natural opening of the flower of his life and part of it was being a movie star.

"He's not a big hedonistic person, but there's always danger around Sam. It's just there. I mean, look at the opening of this play—the kidnapping and the building blows up."

The next few years were barren and confused—as are all periods of transition. Poland assessed that time as a "transition from being La Mama's playwright to being the world's playwright and a movie star." Later in 1970, Poland wanted to move another Shepard play, *Shaved Splits*, to off Broadway. It had opened in July at La Mama and was directed by Bill Hart, Shepard's former roommate. He called Toby Cole, Shepard's agent, who informed Poland that "Sam doesn't want anything moved anymore—he doesn't want his plays called tissue paper." Poland didn't blame him: "He had a triple whammy at the time because *Sidewinder* had opened to a not good response at Lincoln Center, *Zabriskie Point* opened to bad reviews, and he was devastated."

According to Burton Greenhouse, who stage-managed the La Mama production of *The Unseen Hand* and produced its successful revival in 1982, Shepard was very protective of the original productions of his plays: "He knew what he wanted and always stuck to directors with whom he felt confident. It was a close collaboration.

"At that time, Shepard wrote for and worked with a core group of actors like Beeson Carrol, who could play an amazing variety of characters, and Lee Kissman. Both of them got Obies for *Unseen Hand,* which is highly unusual, but Lee had to beg on his knees to keep his part when they moved off-Broadway to the Astor Place Theater. Those two were in a lot of Shepard's plays."

"I don't think the whole thing could have happened if it weren't for the group of actors hanging around the Lower East Side at that time," Greenhouse asserts. "It was a small community and great for the playwrights—comparable to Chekhov's situation in his time. When Shepard left the scene, he no longer worked with the same actors, but I see the same characters still appearing in his plays, like the old man in *Fool for Love*—that's a perfect Beeson character.

"Shepard was hard to get to know, he didn't talk about his feelings much. He was a quiet kind of guy who didn't go around screaming, but he had a short temper. If he didn't like what you were doing, he'd get angry. Once Beeson came to rehearsal drunk and Sam said if Beeson said another word, he'd punch him in the jaw. Beeson did, so Sam broke his jaw."

By this point, Shepard had grown to actively dislike New York and its downtown theater scene, which he considered to have degenerated into something narrow and provincial. New York was radically different from the California of his youth and the America he wrote about. A good indication of his growing detachment was when Robert Redford attended *Unseen Hand* one evening and asked Shepard to write a treatment for a film adaptation. Rather than do it himself, Shepard passed the job on to Tony Barsha, the Theater Genesis playwright who had directed *The Vision Piece,* in which Shepard had acted. Understandably, Redford wouldn't even look at it. According to Greenhouse, "He told Barsha if he wanted him, he would have asked him, but he wanted Sam."

In March 1971, Shepard had another off-off-Broadway success with *Mad Dog Blues,* starring O-Lan as Mae West. A two-act play with music, it follows the mental and physical journey of Kosmo, a rock 'n' roll star, and Yahoodi, a dope dealer. Anything their minds imagine becomes a physical reality, so the play is peopled with such characters as Mae West, Marlene Dietrich, Captain Kidd, Jesse James, and Paul Bunyan. "O-Lan was adorable," says *Voice* critic Michael Feingold. "She has a kind of Blossom Dearie lisp, a kind of Elmer Fudd lateral *l,* and she's a little adorable butterball. Her Mae West was delicious." But with the exception of that little high note, Shepard's personal and professional life had hit its lowest point.

────────────FIVE───

Shepard was a family man to the core, but in early 1970 he fell under the powerful spell of the wild, brilliant rock poet Patti Smith, as yet unknown to the public, and left O-Lan for Smith's sorcerer's brew of Baudelaire, Artaud, and speed. Kevin O'Connor, the actor who had appeared in so many early Shepard plays, most notably *Chicago,* was living next door at the Chelsea Hotel when Shepard moved in with Smith "in this apartment building a few buildings away right over the Blarney Stone tavern. He was staying with her there, and I would run into him. He would say she was the greatest poet in America, but then Patti was completely unknown. Then they moved in here [the Chelsea] for a couple of months. They actually lived down the hall from me. They were writing *Cowboy Mouth* together. He had worked on *Back Bog Beast Bait* and they opened the two plays at the American Place Theater. They were together on and off—he would go back to O-Lan occasionally because Patti would yell out to me sometimes things like 'Sam's gone!' She was quite wild-looking, she was ahead of her time. It really was an incredible match when you think about it. A couple of years later I joked about the fact that the two of them could revive *Cowboy Mouth* in Madison Square Garden. But they obviously became friends later, because of her introduction to one of his books."

Wynn Handman, director of the American Place Theater,

also heard of Smith's genius from Shepard. "What happened was I got *Back Bog*—I wanted to do it," says Handman. "I felt it was short but it's a very rich play, and Sam said, 'There's another play I have now that I wrote with Patti Smith. She wrote her lines and I wrote mine.' I was kind of hesitant. I didn't know who Patti Smith was—she was totally unheard-of. Sam said, 'She's great—she's going to be a big star. It's the most important thing in my career and I want to act in it.' When he said that, I said, 'Fine.'

"They were rehearsing a lot in her room at the Chelsea because that was the set, and then we recreated her room in the Chelsea at St. Clement's. It was wonderful—I loved it except it didn't go on very long because Sam pulled a disappearing act. We probably did three or four performances plus one when it opened after previews.

"The second night Patti Smith came on stage to tell the audience she was sorry but they couldn't have the performance because she didn't know where Sam was."

A few years later, in England, Shepard told the *Guardian* that his no-show was due to his problems with performing publicly: "I attempted to play a part once. Opening night was the only time I did it. I was in a state and ran off to New England, which wasn't very responsible. I like experimenting with acting, but I don't like the performance part of it. That's where it seems to get deadly."

Evidently, Shepard couldn't tolerate the double life he was leading. His wife O-Lan was appearing in *Back Bog,* the second play on the bill, playing the part of Gris-Gris, the swamp girl with mystic powers who gets involved in a battle between two cowboys for hire and a fearsome swamp beast which is really a projection of its victims' fears. O-Lan had to be backstage every night while her husband was going on with Patti Smith about their mutual lives in *Cowboy Mouth.* Although there was an atmosphere of controlled tension, everyone got along and was polite—and, according to Wynn Handman, "Patti and O-Lan commiserated when Sam couldn't be found."

All the control seems to have been expended backstage, however—onstage was a bit more relaxed, perhaps, at times, too relaxed. One night, while *Cowboy Mouth* was in previews, the audience was filled with school kids. According to Bill Hart, who was in the audience, "They were out of control, talking to the actors. At one point, Shepard stepped forward to a mike because it was time for a song, I believe. He yelled, 'Fuck you,' hit the guitar, and the amplification overwhelmed them. They were told to fuck themselves to electronic music from the stage, which sort of evened things out, and from then on it went smoothly. His was a great performance. It was very difficult times then, which I won't go into."

Frankly autobiographical, *Cowboy Mouth* concerns Cavale, "a chick who looks like a crow"—a pretty fair description of Patti Smith's dark and dangerous image in those days—and Slim, whom she's kidnapped off the streets and wants to make into a "rock and roll Jesus with a cowboy mouth." In the opening scene, Slim cries that he has been kidnapped off the street, torn from his wife and child, and forced into training for rock 'n' roll stardom. He protests: "I ain't no star! Not me! Not me, boy! Not me!" Later on, Slim becomes more specific and laments the fact that his wife has gone to Brooklyn with the kid, leaving him with Cavale, whom he both wants and doesn't want. In fact, O-Lan had moved to Brooklyn and left Shepard with Patti Smith.

One acquaintance from those days recalls walking with Shepard and Smith to the Caffe Cino to see a play: "They were having the weirdest fight I ever saw. That's when I thought that this guy must either be special or in the madhouse. It was the strangest fight, almost impersonal. I think it was something about movies. Sam said something like 'When I write for movies, I won't have to pick up the garbage.' It was something irrelevant—that's what I'll never forget. They would walk along, then stop, and one would say something totally inconsequential but hostile to the other. Then they would walk a little further, maybe half a block, and the other one would say something. But it wasn't like 'You did this, you did that.' I never saw a fight like that one."

Though they parted, Shepard and Smith clearly remained friends with great respect for each other. It is also apparent that Smith's powerful personality greatly affected Shepard's style, particularly in such works as *The Tooth of Crime* and the character of Gris-Gris in *Back Bog Beast Bait.*

Patti Smith had begun as a rock 'n' roll journalist for *Creem* and other music papers of that era. As a performer, she became very popular among those in the know for her poetry readings, with which she opened for rock 'n' roll acts at the Mercer Arts Center. After she added Lenny Kaye's guitar, and eventually a full band, she enjoyed a brief but explosive career as either the female Bob Dylan or the female Mick Jagger—depending on which rock critic one read—the irony being, of course, that both men were longtime idols of Shepard's. After recording four successful albums—*Horses, Radio Ethiopia, Easter,* and *Wave*—Smith abruptly retired from her rock 'n' roller's life to that of a housewife and mother of two in Detroit.

While *Cowboy Mouth* was going on, Tony Barsha had the thankless job of directing *Back Bog Beast Bait.* "Boy, was that tough!" he recalls. "It wasn't what I would call ideal. Unfortunately, *Back Bog* is the only of his plays I've worked on, because I love his writing. But he can be difficult. If he's on, he's on; if he's off, he's off. I don't know if there's any solution for it. His material is difficult, which is also what's good about it. You really have to look hard to find out what's going on. Sometimes there isn't a way in and you're stuck. But when it's good, it's inspired rather than crafted writing. He's got more craft now, but then he was much more inspired and like nobody

Twenty-one-year-old Sam Shepard poses as the young playwright at work. (Reproduced by permission of *The Village Voice*.)

Sam Shepard (left, background), O-Lan Johnson (right, foreground), and other actors developing a scene from *The Vision Piece* (a.k.a. *The Body Piece*), which appeared in the late Sixties at Theater Genesis. (Reproduced by permission of Tony Barsha.)

From left to right: Sticks Carlson, Lee Kissman, Sam Shepard, Beeson Carroll, and Bernard Warkentin during a rehearsal for the off-off-Broadway production at La Mama of *The Unseen Hand* in 1969. (Reproduced by permission of Bernard Warkentin.)

Sam Shepard (left, third row from front), Harry Mann (right, first row),
and O-Lan Johnson (next to Harry Mann) in a company photograph
from *Inacoma*, produced at the Magic Theater, San Francisco, 1977,
directed by Sam Shepard. (Reproduced by permission of Harry Mann.)

Sam Shepard (right) and Bob Wilson in a scene from *Days of Heaven*, directed by Terrence Malick. (Reproduced by permission of Paramount Pictures.)

Sam Shepard as the mysterious Raggedy Man in
the movie of the same title, directed by Jack
Fisk. (Reproduced by permission of Universal
Studios.)

Sam Shepard and Ellen Burstyn in a scene from
Resurrection, directed by Daniel Petrie.
(Reproduced by permission of Universal Studios.)

Sam Shepard and Jessica Lange in a scene from
Frances, directed by Graeme Clifford.
(Reproduced by permission of Universal Studios.)

General Chuck Yeager (right) with Sam Shepard,
who portrayed him in *The Right Stuff*, directed
by Philip Kaufman. (Reproduced by permission
of Warner Bros.)

Sam Shepard and Jessica Lange in a scene from
Country, directed by Richard Pearce.
(Reproduced by permission of Buena Vista
Distribution Co.)

else—inspired beyond belief. If you knew the right keys as far as the kind of work he'd come from—Living Theater, Open Theater, Viola Spolin, improvisational spontaneity—you were fine, you could always find it. If you didn't know that stuff, you were lost. There are productions that I can see they just don't know how to approach it theatrically. With Sam's plays, if they're not done right, the play looks like it's awful. But when they're done right, their true qualities come out.

"But I don't like *Back Bog:* It doesn't come together and you never get a handle on it. It's hard to put a play like that together. Shepard was busy doing *Cowboy Mouth,* which was an easier situation: They wrote it, got up, and did it. They were having a good time, until he disappeared the second night— wandered off somewhere—to a friend's house in Vermont, that's what I heard. But O-Lan was in *Back Bog* at the same time Sam was living with Patti Smith at the Chelsea being crazy. On the surface it was amicable, but she was having a hard time which added to my problems. Originally, the part of Gris-Gris was written as a much sweeter character, as an innocent swamp girl, and as we rehearsed it, he rewrote it, creating a much better character. The other character had no dynamics and it didn't make sense, but O-Lan had trouble with this new character. She was right for the original character, but she became miscast at this point. The character he wrote resembled Patti Smith, so it became a whole mess. And I was right in the middle of this whole romantic mess—it was hard for me. That it was all under the surface made it worse. Nobody was yelling or screaming or doing anything like that."

But the tension was having its effect on the professionalism of the cast. Don Plumley, who had directed Shepard's early venture into acting in *Eggs of the Devil* and played Mickey Free in *Sidewinder,* replaced Beeson Carrol in *Back Bog.* As he recalls, the final performance was for the Women's House of Detention in Greenwich Village, where tourists from around the world could view imprisoned Rapunzels yelling down messages from their prison tower to friends and lovers standing below on Sixth Avenue. "They brought some women down to see it," Plumley says. "A couple of the cast members had been partying the night before into that morning and that afternoon, O-Lan was waving to her friends in the audience, and an actor got sick and puked on stage. I left. I walked right out. The ending was coming up—maybe I hadn't done my transformation into a coyote yet, which I always loved to do—but I just walked off. Sam was out in front of the theater. I don't know if he was inside to see when I walked off, but I explained to him what had happened, and he says, 'I don't blame you, man, I would have left those people up there too.' He's always been like that."

Clearly it was time to go. Shepard had loved his early days bopping around the streets of New York with his buddy Charles Mingus, but the pressures from without and within were closing in. He had dipped a bit too deeply into the well of his darker consciousness and was in danger of tumbling in. Personal and professional difficulties seemed to dictate a clean break, a new start, so in 1971 he, O-Lan, and their son Jesse packed up and left on a ship for England, where Shepard hoped to finally fulfill his dream of becoming a rock 'n' roll star.

In an interview in England, he admitted "I was into a lot of drugs then—it became very difficult, you know, everything seemed to be sort of shattering. I didn't feel like going back to California, so I thought I'd come here—really to get into music, you know. I was in a band in New York, and I'd heard that this was the rock 'n' roll center of the world—so I came here with that kind of idea. London was notorious for its rock 'n' roll bands, and my favorite bands are The Who, groups like that, so I had this fantasy that I'd come over here and somehow fall into a rock 'n' roll band. It didn't work. . . . I really wanted to find another kind of thing over here. I much prefer playing music to theatre, but it's hard to find the right situation. Nothing communicates emotions better than music, not even the greatest play in the world."[1]

Despite his incredible luck to be in New York during the emergence of off-off Broadway, Shepard came to think of the Sixties as awful and dismissed the importance of the entire off-off-Broadway movement: "To me the influence of the sixties and the off-off-Broadway theatre and the Lower East Side was a combination of hallucinogenic drugs, the effects of those drugs on the perceptions of those I came in contact with, the effects of those drugs on my own perceptions, the Vietnam War, and all the rest of it which is now all gone. . . .

"I don't really feel that the American theatre underwent any enormous changes as a result of what went down in the sixties. It was only added onto. Generally speaking, the attitudes of the press are still the same as they always were toward new work. Bemused condescension or outright indignance."[2]

England was troubling, especially at first: He'd come with a residual load of problems. He had great difficulties with the Open Space's production of his new play, *The Tooth of Crime,* a savage rock 'n' roll musical fantasy in which outlaw rock stars battle for turf. The Performance Group's production of the same play in New York was plaguing him long-distance. His screenplay for British film director Tony Richardson was never produced. British immigration authorities were slow to give him the lengthy visa he requested, forcing him to return to the States at one point. Often he was left with almost no money due to the difficulties of transatlantic communication between Shepard and his agent and the reluctance of various producers of his plays to pay up the royalties due. And, to push matters just over the edge of tolerable, he was harassed by the English police for a minor drug bust.

Shepard did have some success with productions at the Royal Court, where, for the first time, he directed one of his plays,

Geography of a Horse Dreamer, which concerns a young man with the gift of dreaming horse-race winners who is chained to a bed by gangsters eager to exploit him. In plot and in theme *Geography* parallels the equally grim *Melodrama Play* in which a hit songwriter is pressured to come up with another winner. One has only to read through *Geography* to know its author's state of mind at the time, undergoing a cathartic release from the pressures back in New York to come up with a winner in the theatrical arena, and not experiencing the surge of energy and success he had hoped to enjoy in a new environment. Shepard was an American abroad, with an American's ways and attitudes, just as out of his element in tradition-bound England as he was in the compressed frenzy of New York City. "Sam takes theater seriously but in a fun way," Jacques Levy explains. "It's a different kind of seriousness than the English have about theater—a kind of holy seriousness. In order for Sam to write what he writes, he has to have that certain amount of play with the theater, so he can feel more offhand about it, even if, in fact, he doesn't."

Subsisting on his grants and royalties in Shepherds Bush, London, Shepard amused himself with English pubs and the dog races. He became the proud owner of a greyhound with a name out of a James Bond novel, Keywall Spectre, had a half interest in another dog, and watched over their successes with beaming parental pride. "I loved horse-racing before," he said. "I really used to like the horse-track, we lived right near one. But it's very expensive, as far as actually getting involved in it. Then, when I came here, I found dog-racing is the second biggest spectator sport in England, you've got twelve tracks or something, and suddenly it was like all your romantic childhood dreams come true—only with dogs. So I thought, shit, this is great, and I got involved in it. It's really a sort of romantic impulse, you know. Being around the track, punters and all that kind of stuff—I like that world."[3]

When Shepard was commissioned to write a short play for "Open House" on the BBC, *Blue Bitch,* about two American expatriates trying to decide whether or not to sell their greyhound, was the result. Shepard also wrote a little revue-style play called *Little Ocean* for O-Lan, an uncharacteristically sweet meditation on pregnancy and motherhood. It is Shepard's only play to date featuring women.

At the time, Shepard considered *The Tooth of Crime* to be his best play and was initially very excited about the Open Space production, but he and the director, Charles Marowitz, soon locked horns over interpretation of the play and ownership of the rights for an American production, which was already being rehearsed by the Performance Group. The disagreement was so deep and bitter that Shepard and his agents (Clive Goodwin, Cole's English associate, was representing Shepard's interests abroad) attempted to stop the production. Shepard had hoped for a production at New York's Public Theater with Rip Torn playing Hoss, the character he had partially inspired, the rocker who controls and defends his turf against the Keith Richards type, Gypsy, a newer, punkier breed of rock 'n' roller, but that dream production never happened. Richard Schechner, the founder and director of the Performance Group, had pleaded his case for a production. Shepard responded to his enthusiastic interest but was reluctant to give this play—an amplified rock 'n' roll ritual whose form clearly demands to be set on a proscenium stage like a rock 'n' roll concert—to a group known for their investigative, environmental approach. It was the same difference of intent he'd experienced with the improvisatory methods of the Open Theater.

Shepard finally allowed the Performance Group production and, of course, was disappointed with the results: "There's a whole myth about environmental theater as it's being practiced now in New York. The myth is that in order for the audience to be actively participating in the event that they're watching, they have to be physically sloshed into something, which isn't true at all. An audience can sit in chairs and be watching something in front of them, and can be actively participating in the thing that's confronting them, you know. And it doesn't necessarily mean that if an audience walks into the building and people are swinging from the rafters and spaghetti's thrown all over them, or whatever the environment might be, that their participation in the play is going to be any closer. In fact it might very well be less so, because of the defenses that are put up as soon as that happens. . . .

"[Schechner's] lost in a certain area of experimentation which is valid for him. He feels that he wants to experiment with the environment of theater, which is okay, I've nothing against it. Except when you write a play it sets up certain assumptions about the context in which it's to be performed, and in that play they had nothing to do with what Schechner set up in the theater. You can take that or leave it. It can be okay—the playwright isn't a holy man, you know. Except I'd rather that the experimentation took place with something that left itself open to that—a play that from the start defines its context as undefinable so that you can fuck around with it if you want to."[4]

Disgusted with the *Tooth* productions, Shepard tried from England to arrange for a production of *Jackson's Dance,* about one of his heroes, Jackson Pollock, who had inspired his own "action writing," at the only venue he could *almost* trust— Theater Genesis, site of his first successes, directed by his friend, playwright-director Murray Mednick. Shepard's work on the play was interrupted by trips back and forth to the States, and he ended up giving the play to Jacques Levy. Levy later worked on *Jackson's Dance* with some actors in a space provided by the Public Theater, but he ran into legal difficulties with Pollock's widow. Rather than sue someone he liked and respected, Levy dropped his plans for a production, so the play remains unproduced.

Another carrot on a stick that Shepard never got to bite was a tantalizing opportunity (that didn't materialize) to star opposite Bob Dylan in a cowboy movie set in Mexico. He would work with Dylan later, however, and that experience would initiate a radical change in his life.

One experience in England also affected Shepard positively and powerfully—his meeting with Peter Brook, a student of the great master G. F. Gurdjieff and a genius maker of theater—a master to Shepard's journeyman. Through Brook, Shepard joined a Gurdjieff study group which led him to a greater awareness, self-confidence, and depth of character, both in himself and in his plays. Brook had read his plays and told Shepard he needed to think more about character. In his book, *Meetings with Remarkable Men,* Gurdjieff had once said something reminiscent of the thinking underlying the Open Theater's transformation exercises: "We think if a man is called Ivan, he is always Ivan. Nothing of the kind. Now he is Ivan, in another minute he is Peter, and a minute later he is Nicholas. . . . You will be astonished when you realize what a multitude of these Ivans and Nicholases live in one man. If you learn to observe them, there is no need to go to a cinema."

Gurdjieff had devoted much of his life to passing on a system of knowledge to his students. At a young age, he had left his family and home to embark on a tireless quest for the meaning of human existence, gradually drawing to him various other seekers in search of an ancient, esoteric knowledge. He acquired bits and pieces of this knowledge from various systems he encountered, finally integrating all he had learned into a school he called Universal Brotherhood. Gurdjieff asked people to shake off their habitual, outmoded beliefs, to open their eyes, look inside for self-understanding, and deliver themselves from their self-created chaos by ceaseless questioning of everything.

Finally, man is to live according to the principles of the masters. Gurdjieff himself lived a life of strict inner discipline. He was and is a master in whose presence all pretense crumbles away, revealing the true person hiding behind the mask.

Gurdjieff, and Brook's translation of his worldview into theatrical terms, were tremendously affirming for Shepard, who had been lamenting his own and humanity's fragmented, destructive character all his life. Gurdjieff himself had plunged into his own inner chaos, calling on mankind to seek the truth and then live by it as fully and as consciously as possible. The truth lay in the development of consciousness of self and of others and acceptance of all aspects of a human being. Shepard found in Brook a kindred spirit who was perhaps a little more developed and therefore a source of inspiration, and in Gurdjieff he found a master.

Shepard considered Brook "incredible. He's the most valuable director around because he's constantly investigating every aspect of theater without limiting himself. Everybody else seems to go into a certain area like political theater and sort of narrow themselves down, but Brook continually explodes himself."[5]

Shepard seemed to respect other aspects of British theater as well. He prefered working with English actors, who he felt were better able to separate their personal lives from their work than their downtown New York street-style peers.

Nevertheless, despite the pleasures of working with English actors and the guidance he was receiving from the Gurdjieff study group, by summer 1974 Shepard was ready to trade in the London fog for California sunshine. It was time to come home. As Robert Coe, who later interviewed Shepard for *The New York Times,* puts it, "He learned two things in England: how much work it takes to make good theater, and that it might mean something to be an American."

Shepard had worked through the negativity of the past several years and was ready to encounter what he'd grown up with.

Before going to California, however, he stopped at his farm in Nova Scotia, where he began work on the first of his "family plays," Shepard's version of the traditional genre as previously mined by Eugene O'Neill, Tennessee Williams, and Arthur Miller. The characters in these plays were fractured and recombined pieces of his real family—his grandparents, parents, sisters, and himself—transformed into the Real American Family: the Shepards, not the Nelsons. This initial play was not completed, but it served as groundwork for the two which came later, *Buried Child* and *Curse of the Starving Class.*

After the farm in Nova Scotia, California was rough going. Shepard and his family were living with O-Lan's mother, Scarlett, and her new husband, Johnny Dark, in a tract home near Corte Madera—"the kind of place with paisley felt wallpaper in the bathroom," recalls a friend. Money was short, so Shepard worked in construction. He was still working in New York in a manner of speaking: His plays were being produced as frequently as ever. Though *Man Fly,* another play he'd written in England, was turned down for production, *Action,* which was a response to the advice given him by Peter Brook, was being produced at the American Place Theater, directed by Nancy Meckler, an American living in England whose work Shepard greatly respected. She had directed an excellent workshop production of *Icarus's Mother* and *Action* at the Royal Court's Theatre Upstairs.

Action seemed at the time to be one of Shepard's most difficult plays. It is what its title suggests: a series of basic actions such as eating, chewing on one's arm, random outbursts of violence, with little apparent connection to character. But in its seeming randomness, the play explores action as a shield from the terrors of stasis.

Wynn Handman, the director of the American Place, was reluctant at first to do *Action* without Shepard being there: "I couldn't imagine doing a play without the author being there.

He said, 'Look, New York is a nightmare for me.' Plus he doesn't fly, and he's so creative—once he writes a play, it's out there. He doesn't sit on a play like a hen on an egg. Since *Action* is really short, I asked him for something to go with it. So he wrote a long monologue, *Killer's Head.* I had a student who auditioned for it who did the role, a young man named Richard Gere. He was great." Gere was later to co-star with Shepard in his first major screen role as the wheat farmer in *Days of Heaven.*

Not quite as well-known or as readily produced in California as he was in New York, Shepard had difficulty finding a place for himself in the middle Seventies. At the same time, a San Francisco theater figure named John Lion was trying to start a theater in the Bay Area, which he would call the Magic Theater. The only stumbling block, of course, was lack of funding. Just when things looked particularly grim, Lion found his space and Shepard won another Rockefeller grant.

Experience had taught Shepard that it was best to work as he had first done at Theater Genesis: with his friends, people whom he knew and liked, rather than with careerists, a breed he had learned to avoid. In his introduction to *Eight From Off Off Broadway,* Ralph Cook wrote about the turnover of actors and writers from Theater Genesis: "The best receive money offers and the worst feel unappreciated. . . . An actor finds himself torn between accepting a role in a piece of Broadway entertainment or originating a role which defines not only himself but also his community. The playwright, if he's able to reach this audience, is therefore an interest and a profit to the commercial theater, and is then subject to all the corrupting pressures of an already archaic economic structure."

"That's the attitude Sam comes out of," maintains Michael Smith, the *Village Voice* critic who first "discovered" Shepard at Theater Genesis, "and I think that attitude still rings in him."

SIX

Officially playwright-in-residence at the Magic Theater under a Rockefeller grant, Shepard was finally free to experiment freely without any thought of commercial considerations. In the summer of 1975, a few months after they had closed at American Place, he directed the Magic's production of *Action* and *Killer's Head.*

Voice critic Michael Feingold observed Shepard in rehearsal for a few hours one day and found Shepard to be a "wonderful director of his own stuff. It wasn't that he was any more wonderful than any other director who ever lived. It was that he knew what he was doing and he knew how to talk to the actors. He had a very good rapport with everybody. You can always tell in rehearsal if you have a good or bad situation because it's like in the air. What Sam put in the air was very good—a very free and easy feeling—and, at the same time, he was getting exactly what he wanted without pushing. It's the actors who have to create the thing; they have to make it themselves, but you always have to be in charge of what they're making. He would let them do things their own way and then he would say, 'No, try it this way.' Or, 'That's good, but . . .'—all the usual ways directors work with actors. It's the tone more than the things you do. I've sometimes been quite shocked at what famous directors do. I've seen Tyrone Guthrie scream insults at famous opera singers at the Met. Shepard had a very easy way with it: Everybody involved is a friend; they're all on the same wavelength; they're all doing the same thing together. It was that particular kind of pleasure when you know your business and the situation is good."

As in his theatrical career, Shepard avoided the slick and commercial in his publishing. Michael Feingold edited the Winterhouse edition of *Mad Dog Blues and Other Plays*. "One of the little disagreements we had about the book," Feingold recalls, "was he wanted to dedicate it to Jackson Pollock. His early plays had come from the New York School of painting of that period. I said, 'You can't dedicate it to somebody who's dead—I mean, you can dedicate it to his memory if you want.' And he said, 'Well, he's alive for me, so I'm going to dedicate it to him,' and I said okay. It was fun working with him because you never knew what the disagreements would be about and he was usually right in a different way from the publishers being right. It was a difference of taste more than anything else. They had selected a rather slick line of covers and he didn't like the one that had been designed; he wanted a different sort of cover. I said, 'Well, we are trying to sell these books as a series.' He said, "You mean, you want them to all look the same.' I said, 'No, we want them all to look like the author's personality as reflected through the style of the series.' Those differences can't ever really be pinned down, so you end up getting very convoluted. The compromise was that we used the photograph he'd wanted for the cover as the illustration opposite the title page, where we'd normally put a photograph from the play. The covers were by Barry Zaid, who is one of the very smart Milton Glaser disciples at Pushpin Studios, so you see Shepard's style would be a totally different route. It was the middle Seventies, during the lull period before Sam became a movie star."

Winterhouse Press soon went bankrupt, and both Bobbs-Merrill and Grove Press, Shepard's other publishers, had let him go out of print. In the summer of 1975, Michael Roloff, playwright and translator of Peter Handke, started Urizen Press with a partner. Through his friendship with Toby Cole, Roloff was able to pick up Shepard as a client, and before they, too, went bankrupt, Urizen managed to bring twenty-six plays into print.

By 1976 Shepard was in full swing: His association with the Magic Theater—his theater family—was tremendously satisfying; he no longer avoided his productions because they were destroying his plays. He'd found a director, Robert Woodruff, with whom he had the kind of understanding and rapport he'd failed to achieve too many times. In an interview with Robert Coe, Robert Woodruff told how he first came to direct a Shepard play: "San Francisco has a small theatre community. You get to know everyone, and when something feels right it becomes sort of natural for two people to work together. The first play of his I did was *The Sad Lament of Pecos Bill on the Eve of Killing His Wife.* I'd been working at the Eureka Theatre for about three years and Sam had enjoyed my work—it interested him. In 1976, we were organizing the Bay Area Playwrights' Festival in San Francisco and I asked him for a piece. He had written this operetta for a huge bicentennial project that the city had authorized in 1976, and which was really a mess; they'd spent $100,000 and wound up not using *Pecos.* He said, 'I have this piece, so do it,' and handed me an eight-page manuscript with words and sheet music . . . a wonderful piece which creates a problem as to where to perform it in New York. I would like to do it at midnight in a cabaret kind of setting."

Their collaboration was extensive and productive. Though Shepard was careful not to step on Woodruff's toes, he was always actively present at the Magic Theater rehearsals. When a production would move to New York, Woodruff would carry the result of their joint efforts across the country to the city Shepard refused to visit. Later in their relationship Woodruff commented on how much he had learned from Shepard about "the possibilities of theater. I think, too, that the form I've given his work has been important to him. I think there's been a trust we are both learning to relax behind. It's been a great gift just watching the productions he's directed."

By this time Shepard, O-Lan, and Jesse Mojo, along with O-Lan's mother, Scarlett, and her husband, Johnny Dark, were living together in a home in Marin County, a modest, almost ramshackle suburban house just off the main strip, not unlike the one described in *Buried Child*. Shepard was beginning to ride in rodeos—"a weekend cowboy," as he called himself. He'd taken a lease on a horse ranch, the Flying Y, on which he was planning to raise Appaloosas. Later that year, however, he was to live out a different kind of fantasy, one even better than raising his own horses or hanging out on Keith Richards's estate and writing a film for him and Mick Jagger.

Bob Dylan, second only to Jagger on Shepard's list of rock 'n' roll heroes, was planning a different kind of rock tour: He was putting together a band of fine musicians—not necessarily superstars—along with poets Allen Ginsberg and Ann Waldman, singers Joni Mitchell and Joan Baez, wizard theater director Jacques Levy, folksinger Jack Elliott, ex-Byrd Roger McGuinn, actress-singer Ronee Blakely, actor Harry Dean Stanton, rock musician Bobby Neuwirth, and anyone interesting who came along, like Patti Smith, who showed up looking, according to Shepard, "like a samurai warrior on welfare." This band of gypsies, who fairly well represented the cream of the Sixties counterculture, would make a backroads swing along America's eastern seaboard, playing in all kinds of venues, big and small, not announcing the shows until the day of performance. It would seem haphazard and impromptu, but, in actuality, everything would be carefully staged by Jacques Levy and Bob Dylan. Larry Sloman, a *Rolling Stone* reporter, began by covering the tour for the magazine and gradually metamorphosed into Ratso, the character who wants "access," as well as the author of an excellent account of the tour, *On the Road With Bob Dylan: Rolling With the Thunder.* His opening page capsulizes the spirit of the tour in a few lines: "The Rolling Thunder Revue was a caravan of gypsies, hoboes, trapeze artists, lonesome guitar stranglers, and spiritual green berets who came into your town for your daughters and left with your minds. They took to the road in the fall of '75, a weird karass, Dylan, Baez, Mitchell, Elliott, Neuwirth, McGuinn, Ronson, Blakley, Ginsberg. It went on and on. . . . And they barnstormed for six weeks, shaking up the great Northeast, making a quick foray over the border into the land of snow. Then, with a bang at Madison Square Garden, playing to twenty thousand in a benefit for Rubin 'Hurricane' Carter, it was over."[1]

The Rolling Thunder Revue was to be immortalized in a film, again carefully structured yet appearing haphazard and improvisational. Shepard chronicled his admittedly "fractured" account, the "direct outcome of a fractured memory," in his *Rolling Thunder Logbook,* which, as it turned out, was the only thing he wrote concerning the tour. Once again, the film didn't happen—at least not as planned.

The opening piece of the *Logbook* relates how he and Johnny Dark were riding through San Anselmo, talking about Dylan. Shepard gets home to find a message that Dylan called and will call back later. Not quite believing it, Shepard returns the call and, after a few confused moments, he's told that Dylan is doing this tour and he wants a writer. Shepard protests that he hasn't the time, he's just moving into a horse ranch, but "Dylan calls you and you drop everything."

It was through Dylan's friend and sometime songwriting partner Jacques Levy that Shepard came to Dylan's attention: "Dylan and I wanted to do this tour and do all the new songs we'd written and have a traveling circus. Bob also wanted to shoot a film while this was going on, and find some way to make it work as a kind of *Children of Paradise.* That was sort of what he had in mind—the atmosphere—and having a love story going through it. He didn't know anything about Sam, so I gave him a collection of his plays. Bob read them and he didn't have a great response. He said to me, 'Do you think this guy is really the right guy?' And I said, 'I really do, I think the two of you would really have a good connection,' and we let it drop there. The next thing I heard he's hired a film crew and when they talked about a writer, somebody had brought up the name of Sam Shepard, so Bob called me and asked if we should. I said, 'Yeah, we should,' so somebody called Sam. I knew Sam would come.

"He packed his stuff and he wouldn't fly, so he got on a train, and by the time he got to New York, where we were rehearsing, he'd already written two scenes for some movie that he had in his head, which he thought Bob would want to do. It was a total misperception. They tried a little bit of work on the two scenes he'd brought—I wasn't involved—it was Bob and some of the people in the traveling cast and the film people, and none of it worked out—by this time we were in New England. In this respect I'm describing I may be responsible for Sam's film career as an actor. It was obvious that there was no way these scenes would work, so they started to improvise and Sam was doing it too. He did a number of scenes, he was around for a while—the rest of the film [*Renaldo and Clara*] was done by Dylan and edited by him—but there were these shots of Sam just doing dialogue or whatever and he looked so wonderful— great—and he had this mysterious, cool character going and that boyish smile. The story I heard was Terry Malick saw that and that's how Sam got cast in *Days of Heaven.*"

Shepard participated in the improvisations, but there was no longer a film to be "written," a frustrating situation for one used to writing rather than improvisational acting. It became hanging out more than anything else, so he left and returned to the tour a few times, rather than stay with it all the way through.

He did enjoy many aspects of the experience. The theatrics staged by Levy particularly appealed to his own sensibility. "One of the things Sam loved most about Rolling Thunder," Levy recalls, "was that most people didn't realize that almost every moment was staged: Entrances of people, musicians, which way they went off, who did what, the lighting, the certain kind of mystery playing around with Dylan's appearance— when he would show up, when he didn't show up, what size the band was—all that stuff kept changing all evening long." And the music was great.

But Shepard was beginning to feel like a backstage groupie. He wrote of one concert in Connecticut: "My disinterest kills me. Why aren't I blasting off with them to hear all that music? I've heard it already. But it's not that. It's not having an ax. Being a backstage parasite. Running headless through the dressing rooms. Watching everyone get loaded."[2]

"Sam was miserable on the tour," recalls Larry Sloman. "There were a bunch of us who were kind of outsiders, even the film crew were outsiders. The whole tour was haphazard—that was the aesthetic—just go into a place, don't tell anybody what town. A romantic notion, but, at the same time, there was a bottom line: You had to sell tickets, there was a nut they had to meet every time. So in the beginning there were all these small halls and then, by the end of the tour, they were playing big fifteen-thousand-seat arenas because they had to make up the money. The romantic ideal got lost somewhere along the line.

"Bob was going to make this movie, but the tour was such a grueling thing that the notion of also shooting a movie was very ambitious but crazy. So the film project was always the bastard child of the tour, it would always take a back seat in the minds of the producers, though not in Dylan's, and the film crew were always treated as the niggers of the tour.

"Sam had a reputation of his own as a playwright. He was

supposed to be working with Bob, but he had his own ideas. They never seemed to come together, to collaborate, so Sam seemed very frustrated. I remember one scene in a lounge in Vermont somewhere, this really weird location I had found, a bar owned by a dentist with all these strange curios and knick-knacks such as tables of glass with weird things trapped in them and skeletons in the back room. They all got there and Dylan said something like, 'Let's do this,' and Sam was supposed to start writing down dialogue on the spot. It was spontaneous—that was Bob's idea—but ultimately Bob rejected what Sam wanted to do, and Sam got more and more frustrated.

"The *Logbook* was kind of a salvage operation," continues Sloman. "Sam left in the middle of the tour around Thanksgiving and then he got the contract for the book and came back for the last show at the Garden."

Shepard portrays Sloman as a wild, out-of-control character, particularly in one anecdote in which he describes being taken to a Tubes concert in Boston by Sloman in almost the same tone as Dante related being escorted through the Inferno by Virgil. According to Sloman, however, Shepard took him: "Shepard knew the lead singer from San Francisco. They were playing in an area of Boston called the Combat Zone, which Sam was generous enough to credit me with naming but it's been called that for years. I had been down there for days before the tour hit Boston, so I was familiar with the area, and, as we were walking to the concert, I said, 'Sam, let's check out this Combat Zone.' I dragged him into a place and introduced him to the owner and the hookers, and he was just amazed and thought I was a lunatic. By the way, his description of me was all wrong —I wasn't wearing Emmett Kelly clown shoes, but I think calling me the 'pre-master of tack and bad taste' is a very high compliment.

"I got so much shit on that tour from the producers and the promoters that it was a similar situation to that of Sam. Bob had invited me on this tour because we had friends in common, but until the end I was a real outsider. But I couldn't get past Sam: On one hand he's got that macho cowboy exterior, on the other hand he's got that suburban bourgeois mentality. It's a weird contradiction: Here's this shitkicker walking through the Combat Zone holding his nose and saying, 'Look at these prostitutes, look at these sex shops, look at these weird people.' I felt like I could have been taking William Buckley through there. "He was an accomplished playwright, though, and must have felt like extra baggage after a while. I remember him as very bitter."

In his book, Sloman re-creates a conversation between Shepard and himself: "After a few minutes Sam Shepard walks by. Shepard is a well-known Off-Broadway playwright, and he's been hired to help write the screenplay of the movie. Only it seems that he's been given a bit of a runaround and is seriously considering returning to his California ranch.

" 'I'm pissed off,' the lean, angular writer snarls, 'I've been lied to.'

" 'You're pissed off,' I sputter, 'I get invited on this tour by Dylan, the minute we get out of New York I'm the nigger. I can't even talk to my friends.'

" 'I'm ready to quit,' Shepard sneers, 'go home. They made some assurances to me in terms of money that they didn't follow through on. There's like this reverse Dylan generosity syndrome here. They say that because Bob is so generous and this tour is making a sort of antimoney, antiestablishment position in terms of money and large halls, therefore they can rip you off and it's all right 'cause it's an antimaterialistic thing.' "[3]

"Shepard probably talked to Jacques," Sloman suggests, "but Bob is not the most accessible guy in the world. Shepard and Dylan collaborated recently on a number of songs for the album coming out in June 1985, and the funny thing is Bob never used them."

When the tour stopped in New York for its one big concert

at Madison Square Garden, Dylan came to the opening of Jacques Levy's production of *Geography of a Horse Dreamer*. As Shepard describes the incident in *Rolling Thunder Logbook,* he was inordinately nervous: "Great, an audience full of critics and Bob Dylan. Couldn't be worse." After an ominous silence, Dylan starts twitching in his back-row seat, "as though somebody's given him a bum steer about this whole theater trip he's finding himself in the midst of." Levy saunters over with a "burning stick of reefer, for the pain," but as the main character is about to be shot up with a hypodermic, Dylan jumps up in his seat, shouting protests at the actors: "Wait a minute! Why's he get the shot? He shouldn't get the shot! The other guy should get it! Give it to the other guy!" At this point the somnolent critics rouse themselves—something's happening!

According to Levy, however, Shepard was amused by Dylan's boisterous response and Dylan wasn't "rowdy—you'd have to have been there. Shepard's interpretation of it is as off-base as the critic who wrote from the *Times,* Martin Gottfried, who really put Bob down. What happened was he was really in the play, he was yelling things at the characters. When they were giving a character a needle, he yelled, 'Give *him* the needle!,' things like that. It was terrific, the audience was petrified, not of him, but of everything going on up there. The play, though, they enjoyed.

"We did it very close to people—right in their laps—so Bob was really into it. The next day, he asked me, 'Was that guy from the *Times* right? Do you feel that way?' I said no, and I meant it. I wished more of the people in the audience were doing that. Bob is usually a reticent person, so if he's doing that in a theater, his mind was in another place, I'm sure! As a matter of fact, Sam and I were standing next to each other when he yelled out something, and the two of us looked at each other, giggled, and walked out in the back somewhere to laugh. Sam loved that—that's the least of it—when we did *La Turista,* people were screaming from the audience. They would stand up and some would walk out."

The tour had two outcomes for Shepard: *Rolling Thunder Logbook,* generally considered thin albeit interesting by critics because both its author and its subject were interesting; and the emergence of the Gary Cooper of the Eighties.

In the few scenes of *Renaldo and Clara* in which Shepard appears, he somehow manages to distinguish himself from what seem to be endless clones of lanky dudes in cowboy hats, boots, and shades. One closeup of Shepard watching the concert from offstage is particularly emblematic: His face is impassive except for its intense gaze, boring down on the performance, implying a myriad of thoughts and feelings. It's apparent that something different is going on behind those eyes.

On the strength of those few scenes, Terrence Malick cast Shepard in *Days of Heaven,* opposite Richard Gere, Brooke Adams, and Linda Manz. Gere, Adams, and Manz are proletarian refugees from the urban poverty of the early 1900s who con a wealthy, dying farmer played by Shepard into marrying Abby, played by Adams. There is a brief period of calm, but passions get out of hand and the two men are killed.

Nestor Almendros, the great cinematographer who is responsible for the film's studied beauty, recalls that "at that time I didn't know he was a writer. I thought he was just another actor. Later, in talking, I realized he was a playwright. In shooting, it seemed as though he was doing very little, but on the screen he had a presence, a strong screen presence, what Malick called a 'sterling presence.'

"He didn't hang out with the crew; he was what the French call a *bande à part,* an outsider. He was with his woman and stayed apart. At the time I don't think he took the idea of being an actor seriously. He was professional but he joked about it, so I was surprised to see him becoming a movie star. In movie acting, less is sometimes more."

Shepard was tremendously effective as a turn-of-the-century wheat farmer duped into marriage by a migrant farm worker. Though *Village Voice* critic Andrew Sarris found it a problem that Richard Gere and Shepard "look too much alike to create the desirable dynamic contrast one has traditionally anticipated in the casting of motion pictures," Annette Insdorf spoke for most viewers when she wrote in *Take One:* "The real surprise of the film is playwright Sam Shepard, who creates in his first screen role the most sympathetic, believable, and sustained character."

But Shepard found the experience exhausting and perhaps a bit silly. He obviously hadn't thought seriously of a film career at that point. He'd been suddenly asked to play a leading role in a major motion picture and could only deal with it as a sort of joke.

Back home in the "real" world of the Magic Theater, he directed his new play, *Angel City,* in which he experimented with infusing music into the work, in this case jazz, more than he ever had before, letting it set the rhythms, emotions, movements, and words of the characters. The music in the play would lead, not just accompany, the actors. A loony, surrealistic indictment of the Hollywood dream machine, *Angel City* opened July 2, 1976, with O-Lan playing Miss Scoons, the studio secretary who longs to be a star.

Harry Mann, a woodwind jazz musician, met Shepard when he took over the sax part from Bob Feldman, who had written the score and was about to tour with a rock 'n' roll band. "I didn't think I could do it because it involved acting," says Mann, "but I saw it and did it. The actors were making seventeen dollars per week and I was making twenty-one. Then I started giving O-Lan sax lessons—she was great—she's really got it going for her. [Shepard] had a little reputation at that time, but he was unpretentious, very inspiring to be around.

"Next they did a play called *Inacoma* and the sax player

canceled out, so O-Lan asked me to do it—that's when I became a theater musician. It was a collaboration piece, based on Karen Ann Quinlan, who had been hooked up to live artificially. All the people who were associated on the ground floor —John Nesci, James Dean, Ebie Roe Smith, Fred Ward, Jack Thiebeau, Peter Coyote—they were the hub of this investigation of *Inacoma*—have since gone on to be pretty consistent in movies. The play developed out of improvisation. Shepard had said he was concerned about the story of this woman: He had characters—the parents, holy-roller evangelists, psychiatrists— and the musicians would work with different characters. For example, he would say, 'Harry, you be the musical ego for the psychiatrist.' I would play and she would adopt the mannerism to what I played—a musical interior for the character. Eventually everybody had some kind of musical alter ego which we sometimes used. He wrote all the songs—he'd bring them in the next day. He wrote these great lyrics—sophisticated but regular.

"He had simplicity—you need nothing but yourself—all we had for a set was a bed. Actors improvised because they knew him and they were good at it, but he would alter it sometimes. One time, John Nesci commented when they were trying to get the lead character, Amy, to walk: 'Oh that's slick, that's as slick as snot on a doorknob.' And Shepard said, 'Nesci, I think we could scratch that.' But he would mostly let actors choose their own vocabulary. He would assign certain people in the ensemble to the melodies. He assigned me two pieces, the tenor player two, and we would work them out. It was very successful. He would say, 'Okay, Amy is having a dream,' and she'd sing a song, maybe a lullaby, and he'd say, 'Okay, Katherine, you want to write the melody?' And he'd accept or reject it or maybe we'd alter it. We had all kinds of music—Cajun, jazz, and all kinds of off-the-wall shit.

"The second night we did it, Shepard came up to the audience and said, 'Tonight you're really in for a treat because we're not going to do the second act; we're going to improvise it.' We were shaking in our pants. He put on his hat and sat down. I'm used to improvising, so I know I can come up with something. He just wanted to see what was happening. The whole room got real quiet and everyone was sitting on the stage for about a minute, so I got up and started playing one of the themes in the play about the judges making a ruling, and the other people started getting up and getting into their characters. It was fun, another first for me. It was a really invigorating experience. He was in control but it was subtle. No matter how crazy the characters were, they were soulful. He'll give an outrageous person a soul. When he says, 'I understand,' you believe he understands, and his work shows it."

Shepard felt free to allow the company of actors and musicians to improvise because he was working in a near idyllic situation—with a group of like-minded friends interested in nothing more than creating good and meaningful theater. In a sense he had come full circle, back to those first years at Theater Genesis, when Ralph Cook and the Lower East Side actors knew, instinctually and intellectually, what his work intended and gave it easy birth.

On the more professional side of his working life, however, there were problems. Since Shepard had gone to England, his relationship with his agent, Toby Cole, had grown increasingly strained. Cole had left New York for Italy, which made her management of Shepard's affairs inconvenient. To make matters worse, when he was in England, his work was being performed in New York and worldwide, and Cole's duties were shared with her London-based associate, Clive Goodwin. When Shepard returned to the States, it was to the West Coast, so Cole's assistant in New York was left with the burden of responsibilities and the difficulties of cross-country communications. Shepard felt that his management was suffering as a result, and he had to be ruthless. He left Cole for Lois Berman, who had been taken on as Cole's partner but was now an independent. Not too long after that, Cole retired.

It was a painful but necessary parting for Shepard, who acknowledged that Cole's help had been way beyond the professional call. His career was expanding, however, and he had to have someone in New York who was on top of everything—including negotiations for his next role: Cal Carpenter, Ellen Burstyn's psychotic lover in *Resurrection.*

Resurrection relates how Edna Mae, a woman paralyzed in a car accident that kills her husband, discovers the power to heal herself and others. She lays her healing hands on Cal, a rowdy womanizer who has been stabbed in a bar fight, he courts her, and they become lovers. As her powers and her following grow, Cal becomes increasingly threatened. Because she refuses to acknowledge that she is an agent of Christ and quote Scripture at her healing sessions, Cal decides that she is an agent of the Devil and he must kill her.

In his collection of prose pieces, *Motel Chronicles,* Shepard describes filming the scene in which his character rides out on his motorcycle with a shotgun, planning to assassinate his lover. As he describes it, all day long he rode the bike behind the camera car, trying to keep his mind off the enjoyment of his ride and on what the scene was about. Why was he riding to kill her? Or, more accurately, why was his character riding out to kill her character? The motivation kept eluding Shepard in favor of the fun he was having, so he tried to simply put on a "grim and determined face."

Shepard learned a good deal about screen acting from his co-star, Ellen Burstyn, who was the generating and guiding force behind this film project. She had been impressed by his powerful screen persona, but Shepard's feelings about moviemaking remained mixed, at best. In *Motel Chronicles* he also writes of the isolation and boredom of location shooting: the empty motel rooms, coffee-shop breakfasts with the aftertaste of powdered eggs, early-morning rides in a limo filled with the inane chatter of his fellow actors. One particularly damning poem articulates the pain of a local stand-in, a woman stoned, drunk, and desperate enough to try throwing herself out the window because the movie company is leaving her. "It's just a dumb movie," the narrator tells her. "She said it's not as dumb as life."

In spite of himself, Shepard's portrayal was totally convincing and electrifying. Carrie Rickey of the *Village Voice* called him a "cross between Peter Fonda and heaven."

Paul Sylbert, the production designer for *Resurrection,* met Shepard before the shoot at the Universal studio. They had lunch in the cafeteria, and Shepard related to him his experiences touring the country in the early Sixties as an actor with the Bishop's Players. "It was all sketched in," recalls Sylbert, "and may have been fiction, I don't know. He may have been self-conscious about his credentials as an actor and was telling me he'd had experience in his childhood. But he was very nice.

"I'm sure Ellen Burstyn taught him a lot about acting. She's a great proselytizer and she had a great hand in making the movie—getting it financed and the choice of subject—and was doing a lot of the directing. Dan Petrie is not a strong director. [Ellen] tended to personalize it a great deal. Shepard worked at his role, he was willing to try but kept things very simple. He seemed like a working actor who didn't give anybody any trouble at all. Ellen seemed pleased to work with him. He worked with Ellen in every scene but one, when he's getting frantic and is loading his shotgun to go shoot her. I don't know how much rehearsal they had before, but the work on the set went fairly smoothly as far as I could see. Shepard never pushed himself. I don't think he was terribly secure at that point as an actor, but then he lets his face do so much. I think he took it seriously, but he had no method of work, no discussions with the director about what the character is thinking—he wasn't pushing it. For him it was a relatively straight performance until it had to get freaky and then he seemed to find the resources for that—a kind of rage in himself. He likes riding motorcycles and things like that, so the physical aspects were no trouble for him.

"He is that kind of loner in a funny kind of way. He talked about his wife and kid, Jesse, I remember, and he had gone back with them at that point. It was on again, off again, I guess, most of his life. He seemed very devoted to his kid—that was my impression. He seemed to be concerned and got a great deal of pleasure from him.

"I went out with him one time to a little club in Austin, Texas. He was driving his pickup with the hi-fi blasting—we went to see a mouth organ player, basically country music. He brought a large, red Moroccan leather-bound notebook, at least eight-by-ten and rather thick, and while he was listening to the music, he was writing in it. We were at different tables, but he was making entries in this rather obtrusive notebook. I thought it was rather strange, but since he was not a particularly pretentious guy, maybe he just liked to carry it around. He liked to shoot pool and so do I, but we never got around to the pool hall at the same time. He was studying changing his bridge at the time: He was going to change from the English to the American, which he'd just discovered—the finger over the cue. He's very serious about his pool. There was a lot of shooting around the set—popping away at targets and things like that. I don't think he liked guns. I suspect there was something uncomfortable about that from something he said about someone: The only thing he found strange was that this person liked guns, otherwise he liked her.

"He's obviously an enigmatic sort; that is, he doesn't hide anything, but only on rare occasions does he present anything. Judging from his plays, a lot is going on in his head. It's the intelligence of the guy who works with things, whether it's music or words; it has that feeling—for me—very much out of music. He was quiet, and I don't think I saw him get on a horse although there were a few around. Mostly he kept to himself. I'd see him at the hotel in the dining room—we were all at this little hotel—and he kept music around him a lot, in his truck or in his room. I wouldn't say he socialized much, but I don't either. He was a serious, nice guy. He didn't talk a lot about art, didn't pretend anything, didn't give the impression he would bore you stiff or that he was full of himself. He was sociable enough for salutations and kept pretty much to himself.

"He's such a striking-looking guy, a good choice. I don't think he's such a great actor. I think he's very good at certain things and has limits as an actor. Movies is what you see and his face will carry him through anything. Sam is one of the people the camera likes without falsifying anything—scraggly teeth, too. But it's a wonderful American aristocratic face—it's a face that goes along with the Coopers and guys like that, who were probably prettier as young men than he is. But, still, when they got character . . . which Sam has a lot of for his age. After all, he's beaten the blanket pretty hard in his life, what with Patti Smith and all that, and I'm sure in and out of drugs and whatever. Shepard has a weatherbeaten look to his face. I met him in his late thirties and his face looked like it had been exposed to the weather and a few other things, but it has character as a result of that. I think he does a lot of observing, as well, he is more intelligent. I think that is what the notebook is about."

Obviously, Shepard still considered his true work to be his investigations into theater at the Magic. In 1979, Shepard and Woodruff did the second production of *Suicide in B♭*, another experiment with music infusing character and action whose concern is with the artist, this time a musician, who must reveal so much in his public life that he conceals his private life to the point of staging a fake suicide. The play mirrors Shepard's growing concern over the difficulties of maintaining his integrity as a playwright, working with friends on a small scale, in the face of the compromises demanded by his success as a film actor among a larger community. His earlier plays *Melodrama Play* and *Geography of a Horse Dreamer* also grappled with the seeming impossibility of balancing the three-part equation of economic security, public success, and freedom of expression, but the threat of imminent screen stardom added an element threatening to disrupt the equilibrium of the Shepard–Magic Theater alliance. Certainly Shepard could refuse a screen career, but he wanted that too, he'd always wanted be a star, had always been told he could be one—and though being a rock 'n' roll icon had been tucked away in the back of his mind, being a movie myth wouldn't be too bad, either.

As always, Shepard was able to work these concerns out through the mechanism of his playwriting. Harry Mann, the musician who had turned actor through participating in *Inacoma,* also worked on *Suicide in B♭* and observed the Shepard-Woodruff team at work just as others before him had experienced Shepard and Ralph Cook and Shepard and Jacques Levy: "Because Woodie [Robert Woodruff] was into rock 'n' roll, having Sam there was inspiring because you could see how he would let Woodie do what he wanted, but he would also make comments to me about certain facets of character. I really got into the psychology of performing. Woodie would tell me to do something and if I disagreed, I would go to Sam and say, 'Sam, I think this person has a gentler side to him, I don't think I have to play it aggressive all the time.' And he would say, 'Yeah, but if Woodie wants you to do it that way, he may not want it. But I agree with you.' He would never trespass on the director, but he also listened to what I had to say and advocated expressing my opinion to Woodie. He didn't mind it. For example, he would tell me, 'It doesn't dilute what I'm trying to say about this character by going into that area with him.'

"Woodie and I fell out one time. We were having disagreements about music, his conception of jazz was different. I loved Sam so much because he really knew what was happening, but Woodie wasn't a jazz person. Now Woodie comes to New York and always goes to Sweet Basil. He was the first director I ever met who came up to me and said, 'I want you to give me a list of jazz records.' Theater people can get an attitude like musicians can, and it was very encouraging—it broke through a barrier. Sam being there helped bridge the gap between the director and myself. Otherwise I might have quit the play, because it was so close to me I wanted to do it justice.

"Sam used to come down and play his congas—he'd hide behind the curtain, sit down in his sweatshirt, and play. One of the things he made me aware of as a performer is you do what you do: If you got it going for you, you got it going for you, and you don't make a big deal out of it. It took a lot of ego off of me—that's the effect of being with him. He was very eclectic. When I left San Francisco, I sold him all my records—all of my Bessie Smith, Sonny Stitt, Coltrane. He wanted them and I couldn't think of a better person. He said, 'Wow, man, you're going to give me all these! Look, man, if you ever want these records back, I'll give them to you!' "

Acting in films for relatively large salaries gave Shepard freedom to give full rein to his experiments at the Magic, but he was more resistant than ever to "big productions" of his plays. In fall 1979, Michael Roloff, Shepard's publisher at Urizen, decided that there hadn't been any good productions of *Angel City.* "I thought I could produce that," says Roloff, "and in no time at all I had raised three hundred thousand dollars with just a few calls. It was that simple. I wanted to do the play plus make some money for Urizen. I had Karl Webber, whom I had worked with on all the Handke plays, as director. I wanted to use the sculptor Richard Serra to do the stage set, and I wanted to use Paul Sylbert as well. We were really well along the road when Sam nixed it because it was too what he called "Hollywood"—Paul Sylbert was too Hollywood. He had worked with him on *Resurrection* and thought he was too Hollywood. I can see what he means, but he's wrong. My idea was to get first-rate people, people who are at the top of their profession, and get them to work together and do it pretty big. Once I had three hundred thousand, I knew I could get more. But Sam said no because I was basically going a star route. Once you've raised close to half a million dollars, you hope to get—I forget who the actor was we were approaching—was it Dustin Hoffman? But that's roughly where we were. It was definitely bankable stars—the money route. But the idea was to come up with a first-rate production. Sam didn't want that kind of production at all—it had the Hollywood smell to it. I think he feels very uneasy with that kind of thing, with Broadway."

Shepard was more pleased at the prospect of the American Place's production of a new play about a Howard Hughes-type character, *Seduced,* directed by playwright Jack Gelber, who had stood the theater world on its ear many years earlier with *The Connection,* vividly performed by the Living Theater.

Michael Feingold, who at the time was literary manager of the Tyrone Guthrie Theater, had tried to get the premiere, but it didn't work out because the managing director of the Guthrie created impossibilities in the negotiations, "talked out of both sides of his mouth," according to Feingold, "in a way that made Sam angry. In fact, I still have a letter from him complaining about that, which was the first thing that tipped me off that all was not well. He had said, 'I'd be glad for you to do my plays but management has to keep both hands on the table.' " Once again, Shepard reverted to a situation which had proved in the past to be relatively comfortable. Win Handman of American Place had heard of *Seduced* and went to see it at Trinity Square Repertory in Providence, Rhode Island. "I thought it was a damn good play," Handman recalls, "and got excited about doing it, but I got fastened on one thing: I would do it only if Rip Torn played the part of Howard Hughes. So I called Sam and said, 'You know, I want to approach Rip Torn. I think he would be interested. How do you feel about it?' Sam was like a kid: 'You mean you really could get Rip?' I said, 'I'll get Rip if you tell me you want him.' 'Oh, that would be great!' So I got Rip Torn and we did it in 1979." Shepard was particularly delighted in view of the fact that he and his agent had attempted long and futilely to pin down the elusive Rip Torn for the part of Hoss in *The Tooth of Crime*.

With *Curse of the Starving Class,* presented on March 2, 1978, and directed by Robert Woodruff at the Magic, Shepard's writing entered a new phase. More realistic than his previous works, more accessible, and less populated by fantastic characters like the Lobsterman of *Cowboy Mouth,* or by characters undergoing "transformations" as they did in plays like *Back Bog Beast Bait, Curse* was drawn from memories and characters in his own family. He was dealing with his familiar themes of heredity and the increasing fragmentation and alienation of the American family, but the work seemed more distinct and formed, as if it had been lifted and clarified from his own inner turmoil to a pure and complete existence of its own. Words didn't rush out of him anymore, "as quickly as anyone could speak," as his early friend Charles Mingus described it. His language was considered, more consciously crafted, his characters deeper. The family was not just his own or even representative of all American families; he was telling us about a family in order to speak about the culture.

Shepard's second family play, *Buried Child,* closely followed, premiering at the Magic on June 27, 1979, soon after it closed its run of 157 performances in New York at the Theatre de Lys on Christopher Street. That same day, May 16, 1979, *Buried Child* won the Pulitzer Prize, an honor about which Shepard has been reluctant to speak, but which undoubtedly gave him much pride and satisfaction. Shepard had been given an Obie for *Curse of the Starving Class* the year before, creating quite a controversy, since the play had not yet been produced off-Broadway. Shepard's letter of acceptance, which was published in the *Village Voice,* casts some light on his process and the relationship of the two family plays, dealing with the same concerns, yet quite different in tone and plot:

"One of the things that always amazes me about theater as a form is the vastness of its possibilities. It always seems as though any one play can only hope to be a small fragment of the whole picture. At the beginning of writing, it feels like anything is possible. Then slowly things get narrowed down into this form that turns out to be the play. No matter what the result is it's always disappointing in the light of that first impulse. This disappointment then becomes the excuse for writing another play. It seems to go on with no cure in sight. I'm very happy to receive this award since it marks the first play of mine that has been recognized for itself. Although it still remains only a fragment of the whole, I hope when it's seen in New York, it can serve as an inspiration to some and a total conundrum to others. Thank you."

He was now a Pulitzer Prize–winner and an emerging film star, but Shepard turned down offers such as the role later played by John Travolta in *Urban Cowboy,* as well as chances to mount his plays on Broadway. He preferred to keep on working with like-minded friends in an atmosphere free of the strictures of commercialism.

One longtime friend who had also held to a similar vision was Joe Chaikin, founder of the Open Theater, which had had such a strong influence in shaping Shepard's early work. Shepard held Chaikin in high regard, and, despite the separation of a continent, in 1979 and 1980 they collaborated on two pieces, *Tongues* and *Savage/Love.* In the notes preceding the published version of *Tongues,* Shepard explained that he and Chaikin wanted to work together and agreed to meet regularly for three weeks in different locations ranging from a restaurant to a beach to a truck, and, finally, in a theater. They agreed to do a piece on voices, voices expressing character, expressing emotion, expressing action, just as Shepard and Mingus had played with voices to suggest the personas which underlay and informed them. Shepard and Chaikin met and talked, sometimes writing down verbatim what they had developed, gradually coming to the idea of an original kind of musical accompaniment making use of a wide variety of sounds. The final form of *Tongues* placed Chaikin on a chair, a Mexican blanket draped over his lap, with Shepard sitting directly behind him on a platform. They sat back to back, Chaikin immobile except for his face, Shepard's arms playing the instruments that seemed to protrude from Chaikin's body like a many-limbed Indian goddess.

About a year or so later, Chaikin and Shepard collaborated on another piece, *Savage/Love,* which they presented on a bill with a revival of *Tongues.* According to Chaikin, they wrote each other and talked on the phone: "Before meeting, we decided our piece should be about romantic love and about the closeness and distance between lovers. Our agreement at the outset was to meet for three weeks to compose the piece. At the end of the three weeks, we would perform both the new piece and *Tongues* for a public audience in San Francisco. . . . When we began to talk and work, even though we each had very different stories, we found that we shared many thoughts about the human experience of love. We talked especially about the difficulty of expressing tenderness, and the dread of being replaced.

"The first step was to choose the moments, and then to speak from within those moments. A 'moment' could be the first instant of meeting the lover, or it could be the experience of lovers sleeping next to one another, with one a little bit awake watching the other one asleep."

Unlike *Tongues,* in *Savage/Love* Chaikin would improvise and Shepard would write. They were joined in the final days by Harry Mann, who had appeared in *Inacoma* and *Suicide in Bb,* and another musician, Skip LaPlante, who played his own homemade instruments. At first, Chaikin had objected to the title *Savage/Love*—it implied a view of love antithetical to his nature. "I found something wrong with it each time I spoke and heard it," he says. "But by the second or third performance, I felt the power and appropriateness of these two words.

"*Savage/Love:* common poems of real and imagined moments in the spell of love."[4]

Chaikin and Shepard did seem unlikely collaborators in certain ways, as apart in their personalities and expression as their homes—New York and California. Chaikin had been an important innovator in making theater through group improvisation, whereas Shepard had tended toward creating his plays alone, allowing actors to improvise only within the parameters preset by his writing. Even in the pieces that had developed from improvisation, such as *Inacoma,* his control was subtle but direct.

What they did have in common was an openness to the stimulation for growth that they provided each other, as well as a sense of themselves that accepted differences as complementary rather than contradictory. In a *Village Voice* article by Eileen Blumenthal, who has written extensively about Joe Chaikin, Shepard said, "I feel like I'm an apprentice to Joe, I don't feel that in any kind of pejorative way, like a servant, but—I feel like he's my elder. He's really a valuable man. So there's no problem with me in terms of feeling like his ideas are infringing on my 'vision.' "

Harry Mann, who worked on both pieces, experienced another theatrical turning point: "You don't charge people five dollars for a half hour, but when I saw *Tongues,* I said, 'Man, it's worth twenty-five dollars to see him and Joe Chaikin." According to Mann, *Savage/Love* was a "killer. They nailed San Francisco to the wall—people were getting divorces and getting married again. It was greatness personified." Joseph Papp asked them to bring it to the Public Theater, where they rehearsed an additional two weeks, directed by Rogert Woodruff because Shepard wouldn't come to New York, and coached in their movements by dancer Phoebe Neville. For Mann, "that was a fantastic process. Sam directed it in San Francisco and Woodie hung around rehearsals. He came to New York and directed there. Woodie was the lieutenant and Sam was the general.

"The music was always infused with something—part of the plasma—as opposed to being the cosmetic, so I had to become an actor, which was right up my alley at this point. I would ask Sam about the psychology of it and he said, 'No matter what you do, it's savage—savage love—don't get sentimental. It's mean.'

"It was like a trio: Joe, Skip, and myself, plus Sam when he did *Tongues*. Skip did the part later because Sam didn't want to come to New York. Sam sat in a chair behind Joe and brought the attitude that it was visual: Sam's arm would come out like a Hindu goddess's as Joe spoke. Skip never really got to that layer in it—I don't think he was interested that much, but I got to the point where I could pick up my instrument and no one would see me pick it up. He made me aware of these subtle things. Be relaxed and just do it—be aware of what's happening. Like Joe would beg, 'Can't you give me one small piece of yourself?'—getting really painful—and Skip had a basket with some change in it, and he would shake it in a hip rhythm—the right basket, the right coins—it's not haphazard. It was all subtle. Sam's not into audience solicitation. You believe in it, and you do it. No winking an eye. It was very honest, full of integrity but not lecturish."

Skip LaPlante had been brought in by Chaikin, with whom he had worked before: "I was sort of the wild card because I had stuff nobody had seen," he recalls. "Sam looked at my instruments and went crazy—it was like a bunch of little kids playing around with toys for a while. We spent a long time sort of 'here's a scene and throw a sound at it.' I would pick something up from the pile and make sounds with that. It was really intuitive with everybody—whoever felt like it made the next suggestion. I remember one section I was bowing on steel strips and we had tried it somewhere in the middle. It was interesting and the scene worked, but Sam said, 'Okay, it would be amazing if you would do that in the next to the last scene.' What we found is we had a lot of sounds which would work with any of about four scenes but we'd want to use it once, so we found the one and locked it in and looked for something else that would somehow catch the same effects for the other scenes.

"One of the exciting things about Joe was he was never dictatorial. *Savage/Love* was very much Joe's style of working and Sam was very comfortable with that. *Tongues* was more set. Considering that there was a script, we were able to work in a remarkably vague way. Most of the time when I'm called on to do a theater thing, I'm just looking at a text and somebody's got a really strong, clear idea of how it's going to come out. Working on these pieces was much more experimental. Something would get tossed in the air and it was almost like piranha in a pond—everybody would just grab on the idea and try something.

"The wonderful thing about it was everybody was totally equal in that process. We'd come in, work real hard together, then take off and live our own lives for a while—a real controlled intensity. Sam would just spin in, finish with it, jump in his pickup, and off to Marin and that was it."

As was the case with Joe Chaikin, people from the East Coast who worked with Shepard had limited contact unless they came to him. Michael Roloff, his publisher, never had a chance to meet Shepard until he was planning to attend the American Booksellers Association meeting in Los Angeles and decided to stop at Shepard's home in Mill Valley with the galleys for *Buried Child,* which had just won the Pulitzer. "Sam and I spent three or four days together," Roloff says. "In retrospect, what struck me then and strikes me now—and I've noticed this in interviews with him—is how quickly he'll make the point of the fact that he's really Sam Shepard Rogers the seventh. He'll let you know this within a very short time, that he's not really Sam Shepard. It took me aback that he made a point of telling me that. He brought it up somewhat on his own, worked it in real quickly. It's odd, as though he's not totally happy with Sam Shepard, as though there's some kind of uneasiness about that.

"I think we talked about his family: his father, who was an alcoholic, and his mother, who is a linguist. I had a room in his house in Mill Valley, one block away from the strip. He had moved from a ranch across the mountains. Scarlett, O-Lan's mother, was there, and I left her my brown felt hat from Paris. There was a parakeet in the house who made a lot of noise, a couple of dogs, a backyard like a *Buried Child* backyard—relatively small, not too well-kept. The house was small, neat, no cellar, with a small second floor—like a set for *Buried Child.* I think that evening we went to see a philosopher–lute-player friend of mine who lived in a houseboat in Sausalito. Sam came along—we got along, but we both wanted to leave. We didn't like the people who were there too much. It seemed very houseboatish—way too pretty, something was not right about the atmosphere with the lute and all those things. I was tired and wanted to sleep, and Sam said he wanted to get some milk. The next morning he told me he'd gone to play pool with some very wealthy friends of his, which bothered me because he hadn't asked me to play pool. I thought he didn't like me.

"We had a very nice dinner somewhere with Scarlett, the child, and some other people. Sam didn't eat in—there was no cooking in the house—you went out to eat for everything. Everyone was always going out to eat across the highway, kind of a strip with various restaurants. When you drive into Mill Valley itself, you get a slightly more elegant-type eatery, and we had dinner there. Sam and I went on a long walk once at nightfall around some kind of lagoon, across the highway— maybe a part of San Francisco Bay. It was a very nice walk at sunset, and I think we may have just talked about the ecology of the area—what it had been like and what it was going to be, destroyed nature—a brackish lagoon is what it was.

"We talked a lot about a film he'd been on, *Resurrection,* because a mutual friend had been the production designer, Paul Sylbert, and Paul's very big, long girlfriend, Kathie Green, who's the daughter of Johnny Green, who wrote 'Body and Soul,' was also on the set. She's about six-two and apparently came on the set toting her guns and driving a motorcycle. Sam was still upset about that—by this big blond girl carrying a .45, riding a motorcycle.

"The thing I liked best about him was the way he was with his son. It was darling to see how they got along—mystically, as it should be between a father and son. O-Lan was not there —she was in L.A. on some script of her own. He said somehow at the time that that 'works for me'; that she had her own career, a life of her own, and he briefly alluded to the time spent with Patti Smith. I understood that he and his wife had very separate lives, but it worked between them. We also talked about drugs—I guess he liked speed when he was in New York —I said I had liked cocaine for a while.

"I asked about his plays being made into films, and he said

no. He really wanted to write his own screenplays and he'd done something along that line, but at that stage wasn't getting anywhere. Sam was definitely interested in writing his own screenplays.

"One idea I had, particularly after the Pulitzer Prize, was to see if Sam would write a novel. And he said, 'Well, it's really hard for me to do. I have no problem whatsoever writing dialogue, but it takes me longer to write the directions for a play.' I think we were sitting on his front stoop, and he said, 'Let me show you this. It's in sentences,' he said, I think. It was not a play. And I read it—it was a couple of pages—and said, 'This is a poem.' He said, 'That's right.' I said, 'Who is the girl in the red dress?' He answered, 'I'll never tell you.'

"I think somewhere after the second day, two guys showed up from L.A., novelist and screenwriter Rudy Wurlitzer and filmmaker Robert Frank. They very badly wanted to go out to Utah to see some medicine man who did something with lightning. I couldn't go with them because I had to go to L.A. They all went off to buy this vehicle they needed first—a four-wheel drive—then they all rolled off to Utah."

Shepard impressed Roloff, as he does almost everyone, as "very, very shy. He'll open up, he'll close off. Basically I let people like that alone."

Unfortunately, their relationship was to sour when Urizen Press went bankrupt and Shepard lost a good deal of money as a result. According to Roloff, his partner reneged on their contract with Shepard: "The upshot of it was that Sam lost income from the sale of his paperback rights to Continuum, his royalty payments, the income from five titles. . . . Sam ended up having to pay Continuum four thousand dollars to get his rights back. He was out three to four years of sales, which was about five thousand dollars a year. He lost roughly fifty thousand dollars or more." It seems that, in the publishing world at least, not going big-time resulted in pretty unhappy experiences.

By 1980, Shepard had been making theater for close to twenty years. He had learned a good deal from those who had gone before him: Beckett, Brecht, Albee, Brook, Chaikin. It was time to return some of that knowledge—to "pay dues," as he put it—so he taught a four-week-long playwrights' workshop as part of the Bay Area Playwrights' Festival held in Marin County. Scott Christopher Wren, one of the invited participants, recorded the progress of the seminar in a piece entitled "Camp Shepard."

They met for three or four hours a day, sitting on a lawn outside the theater. Wren related in conversation: "We got together and talked for a while, went away and generated short pieces of work, then came back, read and responded, and had discussions. Later, actors and musicians, among them John Handy, came in to work with the material." In his article, Wren describes the first day: "Shepard arrives around ten-thirty. Michelle turns on the tape recorder. Pause. 'Hi,' he says, squatting and lighting an Old Gold (must have to hunt to find them). I make a few notes. Cowboy boots, blue jeans, blue T-shirt, green and black checkered jacket, looks like something from the L. L. Bean catalog. Very matter-of-fact, except for the reflecting sunglasses. He runs his hand through his hair, boyishly, and asks us what we want to do in the workshop."[5]

The workshop centered around the investigation of character. Shepard explained that earlier in his work he was interested in language and situations, but now he understood that everything "emanates" from character: " 'Voice is the nut of it,' he explained. 'Character is an expression of voice, the emotional tone underneath. If a writer is totally connected with the voice, it will be in the words.'[6]

"The whole workshop was about how you come in contact with these characters, how do you find their true voices, follow, and how you let characters lead the story without imposing your own baggage and impulses on it," recalls Wren. "There was no ego thing about Shepard being the expert. It was very much 'Hey, we're all writers here; this is the name of the game —let's see what we can do for three weeks.' It was very informal and casual. But for most of us it was three of the most amazing weeks ever. Everyone had tremendous respect for him as a playwright. He had won the Pulitzer, but he was living in Mill Valley—it wasn't a big thing: 'This is Sam Shepard'—he hates that stuff, he's such a private person. He mentioned how weird it is for him to be acting, because he finds movie acting a form of behavioralism in front of the camera. He's turning into a movie star in spite of himself."

Shepard told the group that for him, writing is a "journey of self-discovery," emphasizing the need to draw totally on one's experience, rather than something "outside you." As he put it, "Imagination only takes you so far, as far as your experience goes. It isn't a question of having to write about ourselves, but of contacting in ourselves the elements—forces and tendencies —that are characters. The voices of a lot of external world characters are inside you. For example, when you write about a nun, it's not your idea of a nun, it's the nun inside of you."[7]

Playwriting should be demystified, Shepard told Wren. It's not a magical, unknown act, but a craft to be worked at the same way one would carve a chair: "He stressed the constancy of writing or working with an idea and letting ideas come, not waiting for the bit of inspiration because it will never come. At the end of the workshop we gave him a case of these little note pads he keeps in his pocket, which he constantly pulls out with a pencil to write something down—words, ideas, phrases. His reasons for doing it ring true, revealing who he is, his own method. I remember seeing an early draft of *True West* and it is amazing to compare that to the final version of the play. He must have done at least a dozen drafts before it was produced at the Magic."

Shepard had traveled a long way from the days when he

knew intuitively to write from himself, to chronicle his outer life
—his romping around with Charles Mingus, for example—to
let the play pour out from his pen onto paper as if he were
trading tall tales with a pal. "Action" was the key word in those
days, and he trusted what came out first as his true expression.
As he told the workshop writers, that was way behind him now.

According to Wren, Shepard began directing his own plays
out of an increasing dissatisfaction with "people laying ideas on
his work and from wanting to let the characters speak for
themselves and not be interpreted. All of those imageries the
critics come up with—it's very funny because Shepard is very
unpsychological about those characters—they are who they
are." Wren relates a story in which Ruby Cohn, the foremost
Beckett scholar in the world, was lecturing about the final
image of *Curse of the Starving Class,* in which an eagle and a
cat battle for the testicles of a chicken that have just been
chopped off. The eagle grabs the cat and they're both in the air,
tearing at each other's guts, and then they fall to the ground:
"Ruby went on this whole stemwinder about how this image is
at the center of the play and of his whole work, and Shepard
is sitting there in his chair, smiling. The smile is getting bigger
and bigger. Finally she asks him, 'How was it this image oc-
curred to you?' Shepard laughed and said, 'Remember those old
adventure comic books?' He'd gotten this from one of those
things. Everyone in the room cracked up. So, it's simpler than
that.

"His language is simple, as well. It's not academic, but precise in a certain way. When he wanted to hear something we
read, his head would go down toward the floor, his eyes would
half-close, and he'd be listening with a concentration that was
amazing. There'd be a pause in the room and he'd look up and
make a comment about the piece that would cut right to the
center of it in a way that amazed me time and time again, using
a language that was sort of elliptical imagery but had the nu-

ance and shade of meaning that was more accurate than any academic language or any kind of language I'd ever heard. He would talk the same way when I'd see him around, with this sort of cowboy logic. Very understated, nothing different about sitting with him in the workshop or sitting with him in a bar, drinking Tequila, except you feel there's a certain point you get to with him and beyond that it's just a mystery as to what's going on. I'm sure very few people see beyond that. It's not so much that he's keeping people out as the way his personality is constructed. He really is a cowboy, no ifs, ands, and buts about it. He talks about something and just cuts through it in a very simple, unassuming way, without putting anything on anything. There's nothing manufactured about the guy. Every time I see him in a film, it's just like sitting there with Sam. They're casting him because what he is doing is right for the role. He's not acting—if you look closely from picture to picture, you see no one but Sam, down to a facial expression or a take or the way he starts to laugh. It's spooky."

More than ever, Shepard was becoming a man's man, a true son of the West, preferring the rodeo and the fights to literary cocktail parties and screenings. In 1980, writer Robert Coe spent two weeks with Shepard in preparation for an article he was writing for *The New York Times Magazine.* [8] When the two men played golf, Shepard displayed a surprising sense of decorum: "At one point someone threw a club across the fairway to another person and that disgusted him; it was inappropriate behavior," relates Coe. They attended the Sugar Ray Leonard–Roberto Duran fight with Robert Woodruff: "He was pretty excited and liked Duran. He didn't like the pretty boy, the face in the 7-Up commercials—he was for the savage. He had it all articulated: 'I always pull for the savage.' It was a great fight. We drank a lot of beer and he had this whole lavish betting system set up for us. It was an amazing fight. I remember we were just wrung out afterward, exhausted." The next day

Woodruff used the fight to coach the two actors playing the combative brothers, Lee and Austin, in Shepard's new play, *True West,* "locked together and somehow feeling one another's rhythm. In that fight they were so tuned to what the other one was doing it was a complicated, savage, violent dance."

Shepard told Coe that he was still going to rodeos with a partner named Slim, who had a great way of talking. "Shepard could rope a calf, things like that," Coe continues. "The whole time I was with him he had a big bandage on his thumb because he caught it in the door of his horse trailer. He said of the rodeo, 'Some of these guys at the rodeo are really cowboys and then there's these other guys, TWA pilots, who like to come and get their hats knocked off.' He has a deep admiration for real cowboys—he thinks it's a more authentic way of life." In contrast to the real life of the cowboy, Shepard told Coe how he'd once paid a visit to Warren Beatty for advice on his film career: "Warren Beatty was doing pullups on a bar in his doorway, saying, 'Get Swifty Lazar—he's the agent for you.' " By this time, Shepard had a box of screenplays which he couldn't get produced, yet he was swamped with offers for acting roles he rejected, such as the *Rolling Stone* reporter who has an affair with Jacqueline Bisset in George Cukor's *Rich and Famous.*

Coe was surprised to hear Shepard not only dismiss the off-off-Broadway scene of the Sixties as totally crazy, but renounce his play *The Tooth of Crime* as well. "He says it's totally irresponsible—crazy, wacked out, violent—just heaving a bunch of baboons out into the street." Not surprisingly, Coe was impressed by Shepard's genuinely "secret, retiring personality. It's not a pose—he doesn't like the spotlight, being the center of attention.

"I asked him why he doesn't write more women characters. He said he thinks men are more interesting: The real mystery in American life lies between men, not between men and women."

True West certainly explored that mystery—more shatteringly and pointedly than any of his other plays. Through a storyline more accessible and straightforward than any of his previous work, Shepard brought together and explored his two concerns: the corruption of the artist and the disintegration of the family. Austin, a successful Hollywood screenwriter, is house-sitting for his mother when he is visited by his brother, Lee, a petty burglar and vagrant with a vague but powerfully menacing air. Lee manages to sell his clichéd idea for a "real" Western for a huge fee to the producer Austin had been courting, thus calling into question what makes art, at least movie art, authentic.

Shepard was extremely pleased with the Magic's production of the play he had reworked so painstakingly: "This is the first one of my plays I've been able to sit through night after night and not have my stomach ball up in embarrassment," he told one interviewer. "I worked longer on this than any other play. I rewrote it thirteen times. *True West* is the first play I've truly lived up to."

Woodruff, who had directed the play, took it to the Public Theater in New York, where Joseph Papp insisted he recast for bigger names. Both Shepard and Woodruff naturally resisted the change as antithetical to their way of working. Unfortunately, the situation was imposed on Woodruff and he left the production.

At the time, Shepard was busy on location in Texas for *Raggedy Man,* in which he played opposite Sissy Spacek and was directed by her husband, former art director Jack Fisk. Playing the role of Spacek's runaway husband, Shepard lurks in shadowy corners of the screen, almost unrecognizable beneath disfiguring makeup. Actually his character had not run off from Spacek but had been maimed in an accident. Not wishing to inflict his unsightly presence on his family, he merely lurks about, making sure of their well-being. The part would have been a strange choice for any screen actor other than Shepard, but in a sense it was a quintessentially Shepardesque role: dark, mysterious, suggestive of unspeakable violence, and far away from the limelight.

Because of that film commitment, Shepard was unable to do much in the way of support for Woodruff, but he called *Village Voice* critic Michael Feingold, saying, " 'I want to repudiate the Public Theater production of *True West.*' According to Feingold, "he'd never seen this production but he knew that Woodruff was unhappy with the cast and the pressure Papp was putting on him to shape the play this way or that way. He was taken off it ultimately, but I've heard different versions of that. One that he was fired and one that he resigned. I tried to map it out in the article, but you'll never get a straight answer about that unless you were there. Woodruff said that he was increasingly unhappy and that he couldn't get any further with those two actors [Tommy Lee Jones and Peter Boyle], so he resigned. The people at the Public told me he was fired. The thing is, as far as Sam is concerned, Woodruff didn't direct it, he wasn't interested in it. Papp's prestige didn't matter to him, the New York press didn't matter to him. He didn't try to bring an injunction against it or break the contract. He did not refuse to let Papp open the play. All he said was that this production doesn't represent [his] intentions. 'I repudiate it.' And once that statement was on record, he was content."

Woodruff had been caught in an impossible situation. It's clear that he'd deferred to Shepard in their work together, but he had done good work on his own, and did not deserve to be considered ineffectual without Shepard. However, the bottom line was that he had failed on the New York premiere of *True West,* a play Shepard was proud of, at America's preeminent public theater. It may be no coincidence that from that point forward Shepard began to direct the original productions of his plays.

Seven

In 1981 Shepard was cast in the film *Frances,* opposite Jessica Lange, whose blond, erotic-angel beauty and independent streak echo the image of Tuesday Weld, an actress Shepard had long admired, and whom he'd written about in both *Hawk Moon* and *Motel Chronicles* as a kind of ideal woman. (Ironically, Lange and Weld are close friends and once planned a film in which they would play sisters.) The film Shepard was cast in was, appropriately enough, a biography of a similar spirit, Forties film star Frances Farmer, a great beauty whose intelligence and fire were destroyed by Hollywood and the New York theater establishment, which exploited her for their own benefit. Shepard played her only advocate, Harry York, a reporter who was her stalwart friend and lover. "There were three reasons I wanted Sam for *Frances,* " says Graeme Clifford, the director. "One, I wanted an engima, which Sam is. Two, I wanted a sexuality that wasn't *acted,* which Sam has. And three, I thought he and Jessica would get along well together."

They did, but both were involved in long-term relationships through which each had a child: Shepard with O-Lan, with whom he had Jesse Mojo; and Lange, with Mikhail Baryshnikov (a man whose impact on his art form, classical ballet, was as great as Shepard's on theater), with whom she had a small, blond angel of a daughter, Alexandra, nicknamed Shura. However, Shepard and Lange had other, more promising qualities in common. Both individualistic and independent, neither Shepard nor Lange was the type to be held by a conventional monogamous arrangement. Both came from farming families: Shepard's family had originally been Illinois farmers, but financial hardships had forced his father to give up the land and join the Air Force. Though Lange's parents had left the farm, her grandparents had not, and she had grown up in a small town of nine thousand people. For both of them the land holds, as Lange explained in an interview, "mystical realms . . . the earth holds all the knowledge and gives it to you if you are in tune with it. If you are ready to know that information."

Despite her blond bombshell introduction to the public as King Kong's girlfriend in Dino De Laurentiis's disastrous remake of *King Kong,* Lange had successfully thrown off the ineffectual plastic image that had been foisted upon her. Though it was clear she could have almost any role she wanted, like Shepard she carefully chose characters that personified a vision she could support and limited her work to about one film a year. In 1982, she was the first actress in forty years to be nominated twice for an Academy Award in the same year: for Best Actress in *Frances* and Best Supporting Actress, which she won, in *Tootsie.* Besieged by requests for interviews, Lange would graciously concede for the good of whatever film she was working on at the moment, though inwardly she is just as private and as loath to discuss her private life as Shepard is. She invariably appears off-camera without makeup, dressed casually, underscoring her rejection of Hollywood glamour and demonstrating an attitude that Shepard has always admired in women. Like Shepard's stained, crooked teeth, Lange's lack of a glittering veneer only adds to her allure.

Lange began her career not as an actress, but as an artist. She attended the University of Minnesota on an art scholarship, and met and married a Spanish photographer, Paco Grande, with whom she lived the quintessential wandering hippie-artist life.

They split in 1975, and later, when Lange became successful as a movie actress, Grande, now legally blind and living on New York's Bowery on a monthly Social Security check, sued for divorce and alimony.

After their separation, Lange became involved with underground filmmakers, traveling around Europe making small esoteric films. She returned to the States, settled in Soho, and eventually gave up painting, which no longer held her emotionally. She waited tables at the Lion's Head Inn, a writers' bar not too far from where Shepard had bussed tables at the Village Gate a decade earlier, and studied acting. Through her estranged husband's connections she auditioned for and won the Fay Wray role in *King Kong,* and though she was caught up in the publicity circus surrounding that movie, Lange was solid and canny enough to use her overnight success to shake the dumb blond image and go on to a variety of roles and to produce a film herself. That film, *Country,* grew from a newspaper article Lange read concerning the plight of farmers encouraged to take out big government loans who were then threatened by those same agencies with foreclosure when times became rough. In effect, the government had invited these farmers to overextend themselves and then slapped their hands when nature and the United States economy whittled away at their profits.

Like Shepard, Lange wanted to do meaningful work and she had learned the lesson of control—your work was better when you had it. "I don't mean this to sound metaphysical or esoteric," she explained in a Universal Pictures press release. "But I think it has to do with lessons you are meant to learn in life. When you want something really badly, it's as if your human spirit will profit more by not getting it. When you learn not to want things so badly, life comes to you. At this point in my career the stakes are no longer that high for me. I've learned a lot over the last ten years about my strengths and weaknesses, about having power and being powerless, about being manipulated and being in control."

Though they must have been very drawn to each other, both Lange and Shepard value, respect, and draw strength from the support of a family. Around the time of their initial meeting, Shepard had written a poem expressing disgust with Hollywood women, their silicone breasts, capped teeth, and nose jobs, saying he was "heading back to my natural woman." The poem appears in *Motel Chronicles* next to a photograph of O-Lan draped seductively across the washing machine and ironing board in leather jacket and jeans—a siren of the laundry room. He's always come back, he seemed to be saying—but this time it was different. He would leave eventually and he wouldn't return.

Back with O-Lan after filming *Frances,* Shepard was about to play his finest, most definitive role to date, one into which his man-of-the-plains persona fit without a wrinkle—Chuck Yeager, the ace test pilot who broke the sound barrier for the hell of it and refused to become an astronaut, a "chimpanzee" shot into outer space.

Despite his well-publicized fear of flying, the viewer took one look at Shepard galloping across the range in pursuit of his feisty wife (played by Barbara Hershey) and knew without a doubt that he was the one with "the right stuff"—only he could take one of those babies up into the stratosphere and "push the outside of the envelope."

Philip Kaufman, the director, had been friendly with Shepard for years in San Francisco. He tailored the role for Shepard, so that it fit him as well as his ubiquitous leather jacket, and then built it up to mythic heights. He'd cast Shepard because he knew he could inhabit the role, because of "his intense dedication to the manly life, rejecting New York, the taste for cowboys and rodeos—and all with the look of a man in a leather jacket on a horse meeting a jet plane in the desert."[1]

Kaufman was sensitive to the implications of Shepard being a writer, with a powerful persona that he would inevitably bring to any role. He was not an actor in the conventional sense: "Sam is much quieter and being primarily a writer, responds to different kinds of images. He really has an incredible ear. The lines have to have, for him, a certain rightness before he can say them—a ring of poetry of some kind. Lots of actors can take any word and transform it into something, but Sam waits for the word to feel right. It's a very different experience working with him than it is with typical actors."[2]

Although *The Right Stuff* and his nomination for an Academy Award for Best Supporting Actor ensured Shepard would become a major star, it is clear that he viewed this with a certain measure of alarm. Robert Coe, who had interviewed Shepard extensively for his *New York Times* article, recalls seeing Shepard on television during an interview with Chuck Yeager in California during the making of the film: "In the background was Shepard, leaning against a wall, his oil rig hat on, completely unselfconscious, making jokes, muttering in the background with the guys off camera. Every once in a while he'd toss something in. He really liked Chuck Yeager—he was a man's man, a real regular guy."

Although *The Right Stuff* was a success in Hollywood's terms, it was nevertheless atypical in that it had been made by a group of people who formed a kind of community of friends working together, not unlike that of Theater Genesis in the Sixties and the Magic Theater. It seemed as if every Bay Area actor played some role in *The Right Stuff,* particularly in the bar scenes, including O-Lan, who played a flyer groupie trying to land Yeager.

Apparently, Shepard placed none of his various pursuits above the others. As long as they held his interest by providing a challenge and some fulfillment they were equal. If he'd rather go rodeoing than be in a film, he would do so. He remained relatively unaffected by the siren call of stardom.

His new play, *Fool for Love,* had been delayed by the shooting of *The Right Stuff.* It represented another step forward for Shepard, as it was his first play to explore that mystery of American life which he had considered secondary, the contest between men and women. Perhaps Shepard had come to the realization that a divided nature is not two male selves in one, but the male and female aspects of one's self. Or perhaps he was also working out some of the pain regarding his feelings for his wife and for Jessica Lange. Whatever the motivation, *Fool for Love* is an excruciating "can't live with you / can't live without you" melee, full of heads banging on walls and slamming doors, between a half-brother and -sister who fell in love before they knew they shared the same father. The character of the father, who sits sipping on his whiskey as he watches his children struggle vainly to break out of the trap he inadvertently set for them, is another of the long line of Shepard fathers patterned after his own.

By this time, Shepard's real father had become a recluse and alcoholic, living out in the desert surrounded by relics of his World War II flying days, a man of charm and character despite his problems, but a man whose life had been ruined. In an interview Shepard related how he tried to help his father, but he spent all the food money he'd give him on bourbon. When Shepard's father attended one of his son's plays, he was so drunk that he had to be helped in and out of the theater, and he talked to the actors throughout. He had recognized bits and pieces of his family, and so he got up and spoke to them.

Kevin O'Connor, who acted in so many Shepard plays in the early New York days, stopped in San Francisco a few years ago and visited with Shepard at Tosca's, a bar playing opera music which is frequented by the theatrical and film community. "In one sense it was the same Sam, just talking," says O'Connor.

"He was going to direct *Fool for Love*. He was different in the sense of older, leaner, more sure of himself. We talked about old people and what was happening. He talked about what was developing with *Fool*—the idea of bringing the old man character in. He said he had written it first with the three characters, without the old man. He stopped work on it for a while because of the film work and then he came back to it and added that character, and he was working on the ending at that time. Studs Terkel happened to be there and Sam was talking to him about his father. In a sense, he was trying to tell Terkel that his father was like one of the characters in his book. The fathers in Sam's plays are a lot like his father."

In 1983, Shepard's father was hit by a car and killed. At the funeral service, Shepard read some of his father's favorite poems by García Lorca over the box containing the ashes. It was a particularly difficult year for Shepard. His friend Joe Chaikin had just undergone open-heart surgery for the third time and then suffered a stroke, and Shepard had made the decision to leave his wife, O-Lan, for Jessica Lange.

Shepard was fully committed to what magazines were already dubbing "the romance of the century." Shepard had always derived a great deal of stability from his families: those formed when people created music or theater together, and the extended family of his wife and son, his mother-in-law Scarlett, and her husband Johnny Dark. In addition, he had always remained close to his mother and his two sisters, particularly the younger, Sandy Rogers, who was also pursuing a career in directing and in music. Shepard was a true family man. The decision to leave O-Lan had to have come from being very much in love with Jessica Lange in a renewing, highly romantic way. Her pull must have been strong to force him through the pain he surely underwent. At the time of this writing, O-Lan was getting a divorce—papers were served to Shepard while he was filming the auction scene in *Country*—and continuing her career, creating plays and music, and performing. Their son, Jesse, visits his father periodically, and has begun to act as well.

Shepard and Lange's all-American off-beat glamour, their personal relationship, the movie they made together, and the overall seriousness of their work make for a publicist's dream package. And it is beautifully synthesized in *Country*, the story of a farm couple trying to save their land and their marriage. The subject was close to both their hearts, and Shepard endured many publicity sessions for the sake of the movie and Lange.

The film expresses their mutual love of the land and their need to draw sustenance from their roots. Shepard certainly spoke for both of them in one of the many *Country* publicity releases when he said, "I feel related to the country, to this country. And yet, at the same time, I don't know exactly where I fit in. But there's always this kind of nostalgia for a place where you can reckon with yourself." Lange also qualifies her love of the country life: "I'm not saying I'm that much of a country girl that it could be my whole life. I love the process of acting. It gave me a direction in life I never had before. But my grandparents were farmers. Although my parents weren't. We always lived in farm communities where there were an awful lot of people."

The place where they "reckon" with themselves, guard their privacy, and plan their projects is far from Los Angeles or New York. They bought a ranch together outside Santa Fe, where they live with Lange's daughter and keep horses. Lange jumps, and Shepard still competes in rodeos and has added the unlikely sport of polo to his repertoire—although Indian polo, Shepard's game, is a far less gentlemanly pastime than the one associated with earls, lords, and other un-Shepardesque characters. While some might raise eyebrows at the notion of the heir to Gary Cooper's Man of the West persona playing polo, Shepard would undoubtedly consider it their problem. Lange also owns land in

Minnesota—two hundred acres of wilderness with a log cabin to which she and Shepard retreat. Lange describes the people there as "very straightforward. They're not into being overwhelmed. I still call up my girlfriends and visit the way we did ten, fifteen years ago. I see my relatives. I'm very comfortable living in my log cabin. People don't bother me on the streets. And that's great." In New Mexico, she describes her life as "feeding the horses, getting the garden in, or just being alone with Sam and Shura."

It seems as though Shepard has met his match, a woman as uninterested as he in some of the values of our modern culture yet admiring of the original spirit of her homeland: "We have this strength of character," she told one interviewer. "You saw some of it in the Olympics, it's this kind of pilgrim spirit, this special kind of heroism." Shepard couldn't have said it better or differently.

Although Shepard has never allowed himself to be at the center of any of his films, invariably all eyes are drawn to the periphery where he stands, brooding and magnetic. But in *Country* he almost banished himself off the screen, so deferential was he as an actor, and even in the personality of his character, to Lange's emerging New Woman–Earth Mother–Heroine persona. Despite the toning down of his Marlboro Man image, Shepard triumphed in his portrayal of a man who, in the case of this film, does *not* have the right stuff to save his family. Apparently, Shepard even feels he could learn about acting from Lange's example: "Jessica has incredible courage in the face of her own emotional territory. She's just not afraid to go into places that most people would . . . belly up on," he told one interviewer. "I don't have that particular kind of courage as an actor. I can muster it up as a writer, but as an actor it takes another kind of dimension."

Whether or not it is through his relationship with Lange,

Shepard seems to have entered a new, more expansive phase of his life. In April 1983, Shepard met with Joe Chaikin for a third time, to collaborate on a piece about an angel trapped between two dimensions, a character originally in a Chaikin play called *Tourists and Refugees.* Their work was interrupted by Chaikin's stroke following heart surgery.

It was not Shepard's first experience of that nature. In the fall of 1979, Scarlett, his mother-in-law and dear friend, was striken by a brain aneurysm. She underwent emergency surgery, was unconscious for a week, then was left debilitated, without many normal functions, for a lengthy period. The final piece in *Motel Chronicles* carefully details the story of her illness and her family's efforts to help her heal. Told in a simple, straightforward, completely unsentimental manner, the piece is devastatingly moving, and indirectly serves as a paradigm of a real healing process, one accomplished through respect and love.

Rather than allow Chaikin's illness to isolate him and keep him from his work, Shepard accepted a playwright-in-residence appointment at the American Repertory Theater in Cambridge and began visiting Chaikin in New York, ending his self-imposed exile of almost ten years. During the fall of 1984, he and Chaikin resumed their work on the piece at Chaikin's bedside. The half-hour monologue, entitled *War in Heaven*, premiered on New York's listener-supported radio station WBAI on January 8, 1985. Despite his illness, Chaikin gives a magnificent performance as the Angel against Shepard's background of percussion, synthesizer, and overdub. *War in Heaven* is an exquisitely felt poem, reminiscent of Milton's *Paradise Lost*, about all of us—trapped angels who scarcely recall our origins—all the more moving when one considers the circumstances under which it was created: Chaikin had difficulty speaking, so Shepard sat many hours by his bed, carefully questioning him and taking notes, painstakingly working through the piece until it was complete. The piece vibrates with the power of that healing love.

During his visits to New York, Shepard began plans for a production of his newest play, a middle-class, multilayered Romeo and Juliet story which he plans to direct in an off-Broadway theater for the fall of 1985. He will be working with prominent actors as well as some of his San Francisco Magic Theater "family."

Shepard's screenwriting career is also thriving these days, partly because of the great care he exercises in choosing whom to work with, and partly because of his greater clout now that he is a movie star. There are, however, qualifications. Shepard wrote the screenplay for *Paris, Texas* for his friend, German New Wave director Wim Wenders, but because he had to film *Country* before finishing the script, L. M. Kit Carson came in on the project and received the credit "adapted by." Wenders had originally wanted to film an adaptation of *Motel Chronicles*, which seems a fitting idea given Wenders's propensity for making road pictures and Shepard's fascination with journeys both for their own sake and as a metaphor for life. But Shepard thought the concept too literary, so they began with the notion of developing some kind of road movie and it went on from there. They met in San Francisco and Santa Fe every day for a few weeks to develop the story, but the actual writing took a year and a half. Despite its success in Europe, where it won the Best Film award at the 1983 Cannes Film Festival, its critical reception was mixed.

The result was in one way similar to that of Shepard's collaboration with Antonioni on *Zabriskie Point*: It seems that Wenders makes Wenders films and Shepard writes Shepard. Their styles are strong and contrary. The film seems to divide into a first half full of long, cryptic silences suggestive of Wenders's style, and a second half full of long, cryptic speeches by Shepard.

In an interview with the *East Village Eye,* Wenders stated

that "I felt that for me and in the tradition of my films and maybe also Sam's work, we wanted to get rid of this character that he's been dealing with for so long and I've certainly been dealing with in all of my movies. I wanted to get rid of this guy, not get rid of him, but I felt it was time to find another hero and, in the end, it's Hunter, the young boy. . . .

"When Sam and I first started to work, and Sam had just finished *Fool for Love,* I knew that I had to . . . approach what all the movies before had been avoiding. . . . I saw *Fool for Love* and I told Sam that I felt like we had to tell a story of a man and a woman. And Sam said, 'Ya, I feel I'm at that point too, where I can do that now.' "[3]

The storyline of *Paris, Texas,* which mainly concerns a man and his son's search for the wife who left suddenly several years before, seems to reflect some of Shepard's pain over the separation from O-Lan and Jesse Mojo and his concern for the effect that his absence might have on his teenage son. But in the press kit for *Paris, Texas,* Shepard wrote of the ideal lover-partner, the notion of a female psychic twin, just as he used to explore the relationship of two young men, partners like him and Charles Mingus, disaffected outcasts, searching for adventure, for self-identity, and some meaning in the suburbs and cities of "Amerika." More concerned now with the mysteries of male-female love and attraction, Shepard described a kind of fantasy projection which is forever abutting against the reality of who we really are and who we are really with: "The idea that there's an imaginary partner and an imaginary life that's always superseding the real one. . . . In this relationship between men and women, two things are always in juxtaposition with each other: you know, the idea of who I'm with and who I'm actually with."

Whether or not their visions were real, Shepard and Lange seemed to see their dreams reflected in each other, and the ideas of love in Shepard's writing changed: They have become sensitized and more generous, attesting to the power generated when Eros is given creative expression. Perhaps Joyce Aaron's emphatic plea at the end of her piece on acting in Shepard's plays —"I wish he'd write for women!"—has been answered.

At the time of this writing, Shepard and Lange are expecting a baby. Shepard is in the midst of filming *Fool for Love,* with a screenplay by himself, starring in the leading role opposite a Lange look-alike, Kim Bassinger, with Randy Quaid and Harry Dean Stanton in the supporting roles, directed by Robert Altman. The film is being shot in Santa Fe, where Lange and Shepard share a home, but Lange has not appeared on the set with Shepard. It may be that they are jealously guarding their privacy, particularly in view of Lange's pregnancy, but, in the meantime, rumors fly.

After they did *Country* and Lange completed work on her next film, *Sweet Dreams,* in which she stars as the country singer Patsy Cline, Shepard and Lange began planning another project: a film version of the much-praised first novel *Machine Dreams* by Jayne Anne Phillips. The story covers the periods of World War II and the Vietnam War as experienced by a married couple, Mitch and Jean Hampson, their daughter, Danner, and their son, Billy, who disappears in Vietnam. A screen adaptation by Shepard, and the pairing of Lange and Shepard as the brother and sister, could result in one of those rare instances where a film translation of a wonderful novel enriches and expands rather than reduces and diminishes the original source.

Where can Shepard go from here? It is inevitable that he will go on to direct his own screenplays; writing and starring in *Fool for Love* moves him in the direction of gaining as much control over his film work as he now has over his stage productions, toward expressing himself directly, rather than through the agency of a medium, another director. "I would like to direct a film," he said in a publicity release for *Paris, Texas,* before

Fool for Love as a film had become a reality. "Not on the underground side. I'd like to write a script, but I don't want to get involved in a studio situation. I'm working on a screenplay, but it's all tangled up now. I've got forty pages completed. It takes a lot more time for me to settle into a piece of writing now. It's not so easy to dash it off. Form, for me, is always depending on how it moves. If it wants to move in a certain direction, then it has to be a screenplay. But it has been so bastardized by the studio system that it's impossible to write a screenplay anymore, it has to be written for producers. But it's a great form, it really is a beautiful form."

Shepard's talents have matured, refined, and broadened beyond the raw explosiveness of his early years, but he hasn't lost his pioneer spirit, his continual striving to extend himself past his boundaries. Many years ago, Patti Smith wrote of him:

> December 30. Sam Shepard wrote his first play *Cowboys* in true pioneer style . . . on the back of used Tootsie Roll wrappers.
>
> There were ice caps on the waters. He laid waiting for the year to end and the white buffalo to come raging from the ocean.[4]

Shepard has confronted his raging power head-on. Capable of compassion and love as well as ruthlessness, his ability to accept himself is enormous and therefore liberating. There are those who know him who are suspicious of his cowboy-artist persona and consider it to be just that, a persona. One acquaintance recalls sitting with Paul Krasner, the counterculture satirist and editor of *The Realist,* Joe from City Lights bookstore, and Shepard in Tosca's Bar in San Francisco three years ago: "We were sitting there drinking. I hadn't seen [Sam] for several years and he was just getting hot in his movie career. Carol

Doda, the famous San Francisco stripper who used to dance at the Condor for years and years—one of the first to put silicone in her breasts—came in. This guy Joe said, 'Yeah, I know her.' And Sam goes, 'That's the famous Carol Doda? I want to meet her! Get her to come over here!' All of a sudden, Sam clicks into this shitkicker personality and starts yelling, "Hey Doda, Doda, c'mere, baby, c'mere!' The whole place was looking. And she came over—I don't know why—and Sam said, 'Sit down, sit down.' Krasner was plotzing, totally uncomfortable. She really didn't want to be there, she didn't want to meet these assholes—it was like a catastrophe—she stayed about ten seconds and split. Sam had totally switched personalities, so maybe he should be an actor."

But to paraphrase Gurdjieff, we think if a man's called Sam Shepard, he's always Sam Shepard. Nothing of the kind. Now he is Steve Rogers, in another minute he's Slim. One moment a shitkicker, the next William Buckley. You will be astonished to realize what a multitude of these Sams and Steves and Slims live in one man. And it is from these multitudes that Shepard creates his art. He is who he is and apparently cares little for the judgments of others. Early in life Shepard learned to rely on his own strength and adept mind, and in recent years he seems to have cultivated his lighter side, accepted his attraction to darkness, and contained and directed it into his many forms of expression.

His success is his due. As his old friend Charles Mingus puts it, "In those days if you did a play, they paid you by doing you the honor of putting it on. Fair is fair. The point is he worked and earned his living doing stuff that other people took without paying him back for a while and now he's succeeding and that's important."

Though there are always those purists who would like to say that Shepard the playwright has been contaminated by Shepard the movie star, those who know him well maintain that his celebrity has not gone to his head, that he remains surprisingly unaffected. He has changed, of course, in ways we all hope to as we gain experience. "He changed because he was a pretty wild character," one old friend from the Sixties asserts. "He could do anything wrong and the whole structure would come out and support him and he'd come out ahead. He was one of those types of people with a certain magical quality about him. He's always been smart and he's always been lucky. He wasn't contained, so he's lucky to be alive in some ways because he was playing with a lot of heavy stuff and he was probably close to overdoing it many times—going out there and losing it." But Shepard has always known to pull back just at the edge and to ground himself through his work and through family and friends. He has never faced the vagaries of fame and fortune unprotected.

In one essential way, Shepard has not changed. The work always comes first and even in that area of his life he is restless, abhorrent of routine, almost compelled to conquer new territories through exploring his creativity in a variety of media from writing to acting to directing to composing and playing music, even to sculpting. Yet all his parts fit seamlessly into one smoothly integrated persona. Whether or not that persona is a true outer expression of his inner self, only he knows. Whether any of us ever achieve that level of integration is the real question. Perhaps, as Mingus describes it, "trying to be a person means before the mold sets you can wriggle around a bit, before you're totally fixed in this role." Perhaps Shepard prefers to wriggle in the mold rather than suffer the fate of most of us: being set. At any rate, why not accept the possibility that as he appears, so he is.

Village Voice critic Michael Feingold neatly describes that appearance and links the vision of Shepard the writer to the persona of Shepard the screen icon: "A simple cowboy lost in our insane urban society, at heart he may be more frightened than anyone else by the sensitivity of his perceptions, the lucidity of his thoughts. The tension in Shepard's paradoxical self—the mind of a Kafka trapped in the body of a Jimmy Stewart—probably explains the triumphant success of his screen persona. . . . Everything the movies are busy declining to say out loud about the pioneer spirit as a vehicle for its own corruption, about the cult of the rugged individualist as a recourse for the frightened and sensitive, about a close relation with Nature as a tactic for suppressing one's human consciousness—is summed up in the lingering close-ups of Shepard's face, handsome and expressionless, but plainly quivering with *agenbite of inwit* at every pore."[5]

Perhaps Shepard's greatest creation is that persona. No matter how uncomfortable he is at the awareness that his youthful fantasy has been realized, it seems unlikely that stardom caught Shepard off guard. His awareness of human nature and of himself is too shrewd and profound; he knows that we create ourselves from a composite of who we *might* really be (as best we can discover) and who others wish we were, that is, from impressions transmitted, received, and interpreted. All his life Shepard has been drawn to the notions of myths and mystery, of slipping undetected in and out of roles in a kind of psychic sleight of hand, changing colors with the environment, protecting oneself by seeing things through another's eyes. And all his life, people have been irresistibly drawn to his chameleon allure, his own peculiar take on archetypal American good looks. Now the movie camera has fallen in love as well, and the effect is multiplied.

Self-creation does not, in Shepard's case, signify fabrication. He is self-aware rather than self-conscious, a learner from life rather than from the university, a man who has the courage to look into himself, accept what he finds, and, for the most part, keep it to himself. This is why he did not burn out as so many young talents do, and it is also why he is able to keep progressing.

The objective of the alchemical quest is to produce health and longevity, to transmute base metals into gold, and to produce the elixir of immortality. This can be viewed as a metaphor for the artistic quest. The object of art is ultimate and total health in the sense that the artist experiences the healing powers of the creative flow on all levels of his being; art transforms base life into the gold of insight, awareness, and enlightenment; and art is as close as we humans can come to an existence beyond our mortal limits. To make art, therefore, is to work at being as fully realized and as consciously alive as possible.

Shepard has lived, learned, and tried to change what needed to be changed. But it is apparent that in certain respects he is the same precocious talent who understood earlier than most that creating art is a journey of self-discovery, and that it is the task of the conscious man to know himself through good work. As his friend Bill Hart puts it, "He just wants to be a complete person and do his work well."

One young actress, a longtime idolizer of Shepard, finally had the opportunity to meet him in the summer of 1983: "He's just like us," she reported in amazement. "He's a worker."

Notes

CHAPTER ONE

1. Sam Shepard, *Rolling Thunder Logbook* (New York: Viking Press, 1977).

2. Shepard, *Hawk Moon* (New York: Performing Arts Journal Publications, 1973).

3. Robert Coe, "Saga of Sam Shepard," *The New York Times Magazine* (Nov. 23, 1980).

4. Shepard, "The Curse of the Raven's Black Feather," *Hawk Moon.*

5. December 1977.

6. Shepard, "The Escapes of Buster Keaton," *Hawk Moon.*

7. Shepard, "Where Does a Hero Live?" *Hawk Moon.*

8. Shepard, *Motel Chronicles* (San Francisco: City Lights Books, 1982).

9. Shepard, *Angel City,* in *Fool for Love and Other Plays* (New York: Bantam Books, 1984). Speech is by Miss Scoons.

CHAPTER TWO

1. Shepard, *Motel Chronicles.*

2. Shepard, "Sleeping at the Wheel," *Hawk Moon.*

3. Kenneth Chubb and the editors of *Theatre Quarterly,* "Metaphors, Mad Dogs, and Old Time Cowboys: Interview with Sam Shepard," in Bonnie Marranca, ed., *American Dreams: The Imagination of Sam Shepard* (New York: Performing Arts Journal Publications, 1981).

4. Chubb.

5. Chubb.

6. Chubb.

7. Chubb.

8. Shepard, "And So Does Your Mother," *Hawk Moon*.

9. Chubb.

10. Shepard, *Rolling Thunder Logbook*.

11. Shepard, *Motel Chronicles*.

12. Albert Poland and Bruce Mailman, *The Off-Off Broadway Book* (New York: Bobbs-Merrill, 1972).

13. Poland.

14. Poland.

15. Chubb.

CHAPTER THREE

1. Chubb.

2. Chubb.

3. Chubb.

4. Chubb.

5. Chubb.

6. Chubb.

7. Chubb.

8. Chubb.

9. Joyce Aaron, "Clues in a Memory," in Marranca, ed., *American Dreams*.

10. Aaron.

11. Aaron.

12. Elizabeth Hardwick, "Introduction," in Shepard, *La Turista* (New York: Bobbs-Merrill, 1968).

13. Chubb.

14. Shepard, *Motel Chronicles.*

CHAPTER FOUR

1. Chubb.

2. Shepard, "Language, Visualization and the Inner Library," in Marranca, ed., *American Dream.*

CHAPTER FIVE

1. Chubb.

2. Shepard, "Experimental Theatre: Then and Now," in Marranca, ed., *American Dreams.*

3. Chubb.

4. Chubb.

5. Chubb.

CHAPTER SIX

1. Larry Sloman, *On the Road with Bob Dylan: Rolling with the Thunder* (New York: Bantam Books, 1978).

2. Shepard, *Rolling Thunder Logbook.*

3. Sloman.

4. *Sam Shepard: Seven Plays* (New York: Bantam Books, 1981).

5. Scott Christopher Wren, "Camp Shepard," *West Coast Plays* (Berkeley), 1980.

6. Wren.

7. Wren.

8. November 23, 1980.

CHAPTER SEVEN

1. David Thomson, "Shepard," *Film Comment* (May 1983).

2. Thomson.

3. Helen Knode, "At Long Last Love: Wim Wenders," *East Village Eye,* November 1984.

4. Patti Smith, "Sam Shepard: 9 Random Years [7+ 2]."

5. *Village Voice,* February 12, 1979.

Selected Bibliography

Aaron, Joyce. "Clues in a Memory." In *American Dreams: The Imagination of Sam Shepard,* edited by Bonnie Marranca. New York: Performing Arts Journal, 1981.

Albee, Edward. *"Icarus's Mother." Village Voice,* November 25, 1965.

Blumenthal, Eileen. "Sam Shepard and Joseph Chaikin: Speaking in Tongues." In *American Dreams: The Imagination of Sam Shepard,* edited by Bonnie Marranca. New York: Performing Arts Journal, 1981.

Boyd, Blanche McCrary. "The Natural." *American Film Magazine,* October 1984.

Chubb, Kenneth, and the editors of *Theatre Quarterly.* "Metaphors, Mad Dogs and Old Time Cowboys: Interview with Sam Shepard." In *American Dreams: The Imagination of Sam Shepard,* edited by Bonnie Marranca. New York: Performing Arts Journal, 1981.

Coe, Robert. "Saga of Sam Shepard." *New York Times,* November 23, 1980.

Eder, Richard. "Sam Shepard's Obsession Is America." *New York Times,* March 4, 1979.

Feingold, Michael. "Papp's *True West* False, Says Shepard." *Village Voice,* December 24–30, 1980.

Freedman, Samuel G. "Theater Rebels of 60's Gather to Reminisce." *New York Times,* November 15, 1984.

Gussow, Mel. "The Deeply American Roots of Sam Shepard's Plays." *New York Times,* January 2, 1979.

Hardwick, Elizabeth. "An Introduction: *La Turista."* In *American Dreams: The Imagination of Sam Shepard,* edited by Bonnie Marranca. New York: Performing Arts Journal, 1981.

Kakutani, Michiko. "Myths, Dreams, Realities—Sam Shepard's America." *New York Times,* January 29, 1984.

Knode, Helen. "At Long Last Love: Wim Wenders." *East Village Eye,* November 1984.

Marranca, Bonnie, ed. *American Dreams: The Imagination of Sam Shepard.* New York: Performing Arts Journal, 1981.

Oppenheimer, Helen, and Fascio, Victor. "The Most Promising Playright in America Today Is Sam Shepard." *Village Voice,* October 27, 1975.

Poland, Albert. *The Off-Off Broadway Book.* New York: Bobbs-Merrill, 1972.

Sloman, Larry. *On the Road with Bob Dylan: Rolling with the Thunder.* New York: Bantam Books, 1978.

Smith, Michael. *"Icarus's Mother." Village Voice,* December 2, 1966.

Shepard, Sam. *Chicago and Other Plays.* New York: Urizen Books, 1981.

———. *Fool for Love and Other Plays.* New York: Bantam Books, 1984.

———. *Four Two-Act Plays.* New York: Urizen Books, 1980.

———. *Hawk Moon.* New York: Performing Arts Journal, 1981.

———. *Motel Chronicles.* San Francisco: City Lights Books, 1982.

———. *Rolling Thunder Logbook.* New York: Viking Press, 1977.

———. *Seven Plays.* New York: Bantam Books, 1981.

———. *The Unseen Hand and Other Plays.* New York: Urizen Books, 1981.

Stasio, Marilyn. "Sam Shepard: An Outlaw Comes Home." *After Dark,* January 1980.

Thomson, David. "Shepard." *American Film,* 1983.

Wetzsteon, Ross. "The Genius of Sam Shepard." *New York,* November 24, 1980.

Wren, Scott Christopher. "Camp Shepard: Exploring the Geography of Character." *West Coast Plays,* 1980.

Works by Sam Shepard

STAGE PLAYS

Cowboys (early version of *Cowboys #2*)
First performance: Theater Genesis, New York, 10/16/64
Director: Ralph Cook

Rock Garden
First performance: Theater Genesis, New York, 10/16/64
Director: Ralph Cook

Up to Thursday
First performance: Theater 65, Playwrights' Theater, New York, 1/10/65

Dog
First performance: La Mama, New York, 2/10/65

Rocking Chair
First performance: La Mama, New York, 2/10/65

Chicago
First performance: Theater Genesis, New York, 4/16/65
Director: Ralph Cook

Icarus's Mother
First Performance: Caffe Cino, New York, 11/16/65
Director: Michael Smith

4-H Club
First performance: Theater 65, New York, 1965

Fourteen Hundred Thousand
First performance: Firehouse Theater, Minneapolis, 1966
Director: Sydney Schubert Walter

Red Cross
First performance: Judson Poets' Theater, New York, 4/28/68
Director: Jacques Levy

La Turista
First Performance: American Place Theater, New York, 3/4/67
Director: Jacques Levy

Melodrama Play
First performance: La Mama, New York, 5/18/67
Director: Tom O'Horgan

Cowboys # 2
First performance: Mark Taper Forum, Los Angeles, 11/67
Director: Edward Parone

Forensic and the Navigators
First performance: Theater Genesis, New York, 12/29/67
Director: Ralph Cook

Holy Ghostly
First performance: New Troupe branch of La Mama (on tour), 1969
Director: Tom O'Horgan

The Unseen Hand
First performance: La Mama, New York, 12/26/69
Director: Jeff Blechner

Operation Sidewinder
First performance: Repertory Theater of Lincoln Center, New York, 3/12/70
Director: Michael A. Schultz

Shaved Splits
First performance: La Mama, New York, 7/20/70
Director: Bill Hart

Mad Dog Blues
First performance: Theater Genesis, New York, 3/4/71
Director: Robert Glaudini

Cowboy Mouth (with **Patti Smith**)
First performance: Traverse Theatre, Edinburgh, 4/12/71
Director: Gordon Stewart

Back Bog Beast Bait
First performance: American Place Theater, New York, 4/29/71
Director: Tony Barsha

The Tooth of Crime
First performance: Open Space Theatre, London, 7/17/72
Director: Charles Marowitz, assisted by Walter Donohue

Blue Bitch
First performance: "Open House," BBC television, spring 1973

Geography of a Horse Dreamer
First performance: Theatre Upstairs (Royal Court), London, 2/22/74
Director: Sam Shepard

Little Ocean
First performance: Hampstead Theatre Club, London, 3/25/74
Director: Stephen Rae

Action and *Killer's Head*
First performance: American Place Theater, New York, 1975
Director: Nancy Meckler

Man Fly (**unproduced**)

Jackson's Dance (**unproduced**)

Angel City
First performance: Magic Theater, San Francisco, 7/2/76
Director: Sam Shepard

Suicide in B♭
First performance: Yale Repertory Theater, New Haven, 10/15/76
Director: Walt Jones and Denise A. Gordon

Inacoma
First performance: Magic Theater, San Francisco, 1977

The Sad Lament of Pecos Bill on the Eve of Killing His Wife
First Performance: San Francisco, 1978

Tongues (with Joe Chaikin)
First performance: Magic Theater, San Francisco, 1978

Curse of the Starving Class
First performance: New York Shakespeare Festival, New York, 3/2/78
Director: Robert Woodruff

Savage/Love (with Joe Chaikin)
First performance: Magic Theater, San Francisco, 1979

Buried Child
First performance: Magic Theater, San Francisco, 6/27/79
Director: Robert Woodruff

Seduced
First performance: American Place Theater, New York, 1979
Director: Jack Gelber

True West
First performance: Magic Theater, San Francisco, 7/10/80
Director: Robert Woodruff

Fool for Love
First Performance: Magic Theater, San Francisco, 2/8/83
Director: Sam Shepard

War in Heaven (with Joe Chaikin)
First performance: WBAI radio, New York, 1/8/85

SCREENPLAYS:

Me and My Brother (with Robert Frank)
Zabriskie Point (with Michelangelo Antonioni and others)
Ringaleevio (with Murray Mednick; unproduced)
Maxagasm (unproduced)
Bodyguard (unproduced)
Paris, Texas (dir. Wim Wenders, with Harry Dean Stanton, Nastassia Kinski)
Fool for Love (dir. Robert Altman, with Sam Shepard, Kim Bassinger, Randy Quaid, Harry Dean Stanton)

SHORT STORIES AND POEMS

Hawk Moon. Los Angeles: Black Sparrow Press, 1973; reprinted New York: Performing Arts Journal, 1981.
Rolling Thunder Logbook. New York: Viking Press, 1977.
Motel Chronicles. San Francisco: City Lights Books, 1982.

SCREEN ROLES

Renaldo and Clara (1978), written and directed by Bob Dylan, with Bob Dylan, Joan Baez, Bob Neuwirth, Ronee Blakley, Sara Dylan, Allen Ginsberg, Jack Elliott, David Blue, Helena Kallianotes, Ruth Tyraniel, Harry Dean Stanton, Steven Soles, Rob Stoner, Roger McGuinn, Anne Waldman, Mick Ronson, Ronnie Hawkins, Denise Mercedes, Linda Thomases, Scarlet Rivera, David Mansfield, Howie Wyeth, Luther Rix, T-Bone Burnett
Days of Heaven (1978), directed by Terrence Malick, with Richard Gere, Brooke Adams, Linda Ganz
Resurrection (1980), directed by Daniel Petrie, with Ellen Burstyn, Eva Le Gallienne, Roberts Blossom

Frances (1982), directed by Graeme Clifford, with Jessica Lange, Kim Stanley

Raggedy Man (1981), directed by Jack Fisk, with Sissy Spacek, Eric Roberts

The Right Stuff (1983), directed by Philip Kaufman, with Dennis Quaid, Fred Ward, Ed Harris, Scott Paulin, Charles Frank, Lance Henriksens, Scott Glenn, Barbara Hershey, Kim Stanley

Country (1984), directed by Richard Pearce, with Jessica Lange

Fool for Love (1985), directed by Robert Altman, with Kim Bassinger, Randy Quaid, Harry Dean Stanton

INDEX

Aaron, Joyce, 38, 45–49, 52, 53, 55, 56, 57, 61, 63, 67, 153
Academy Awards, 1, 142, 145
Action, 101–102, 103, 167
action writing, 44, 98
Albee, Edward, 28, 37, 38, 133
American Hurrah, 51–52
American Place Theater, 45, 55, 56, 89, 102, 103, 123
American Repertory Theater, 150
Angel City, 9, 75, 114, 122–123, 167
Antonioni, Michelangelo, 69, 70–71, 72, 151
Astor Place Theater, 79, 81, 82–83, 86

Back Bog Beast Bait, 80, 89, 90, 92, 93–94, 124, 167
Barnes, Clive, 81
Barsha, Tony, 64–65, 84, 87, 92–93
Bassinger, Kim, 153
Bay Area Playwrights' Festival, 105, 133
BBC, 96
Berman, Lois, 117
Bishop's Company, 18, 20, 118
Bleckner, Jeff, 79, 80, 81, 83
"Blind Rage," 74
Blue Bitch, 97, 167
Bobbs-Merrill, 61, 68, 104
Bodyguard, 75, 169
Brook, Peter, 99, 100, 102, 133
Buried Child, 1, 3, 101, 106, 124–125, 130, 168
Burstyn, Ellen, 117, 118

Cafe La Mama, 22, 26, 29, 34, 37, 40, 58, 69, 79, 81, 82, 85, 86
touring group, 41, 58–59

Caffe Cino, 22, 26, 34, 43
Cannes Film Festival award, 151
Carrol, Beeson, 68, 82, 86, 93
Chaiken, Joe, 28, 45, 49, 62, 125–126, 127, 128, 129, 133, 147, 150
Cherry Lane Theater, 28, 38
Chicago, 38, 39–40, 41, 45, 56, 58, 78, 89, 165
Cino, Joe, 26, 29
Coe, Robert, 2, 67, 100, 105, 136, 145
Cole, Toby, 61, 70, 79, 80, 85, 97, 105, 116, 117
Continuum, 132
Cook, Ralph, 28–29, 32, 36, 41, 42, 67, 102, 116, 121
Country, 143, 147, 148, 149, 151, 153, 170
Cowboy Mouth, 89, 90, 91, 92, 93, 124, 167
Cowboys, 30, 31, 32–33, 40, 58, 154, 165
Cowboys #2, 31, 62–63, 166
Curse of the Starving Class, 101, 124, 125, 135, 168

Dark, Johnny, 101, 106, 147
Days of Heaven, 3, 102, 108, 113–114, 169
directing, 44, 80, 81, 95–96, 103–104, 135, 139, 153
Dog, 37, 58, 165
Dylan, Bob, 2, 20, 35, 92, 99, 106, 107–108, 109, 110–111, 112

Eggs of the Devil, The, 23, 77, 93
environmental theater, 97–98